ISSUES THAT CONCERN YOU

Teen Pregnancy

Heidi Williams, *Book Editor*

GREENHAVEN PRESS

A part of Gale, Cengage Learning

GALE
CENGAGE Learning™

Detroit • New York • San Francisco • New Haven, Conn • Waterville, Maine • London

Christine Nasso, *Publisher*
Elizabeth Des Chenes, *Managing Editor*

For more information, contact:
Greenhaven Press
27500 Drake Rd.
Farmington Hills, MI 48331-3535
Or you can visit our Internet site at gale.cengage.com

For product information and technology assistance, contact us at

Gale Customer Support, 1-800-877-4253
For permission to use material from this text or product, submit all requests online at www.cengage.com/permissions

Further permissions questions can be e-mailed to permissionrequest@cengage.com

Articles in Greenhaven Press anthologies are often edited for length to meet page requirements. In addition, original titles of these works are changed to clearly present the main thesis and to explicitly indicate the author's opinion. Every effort is made to ensure that Greenhaven Press accurately reflects the original intent of the authors. Every effort has been made to trace the owners of copyrighted material.

Image copyright Opla, 2009. Used under license from Shutterstock.com

LIBRARY OF CONGRESS CATALOGING-IN-PUBLICATION DATA

Teen pregnancy / Heidi Williams, book editor.
  p. cm. -- (Issues that concern you)
 Includes bibliographical references and index.
 ISBN 978-0-7377-4498-9 (hardcover)
1. Teenage pregnancy--Juvenile literature. 2. Sex instruction for teenagers--Juvenile literature. 3. Abortion--Juvenile literature. I. Williams, Heidi.
 HQ759.4.T4218 2009
 305.70835--dc22

                                                                2009018274

Printed in the United States of America
2 3 4 5 6 7 13 12 11 10 09

CONTENTS

W hether debating free condoms in schools, the merits or failures of abstinence-only sex education, the "morning-after pill," abortion, or parental notification rights, conservative and liberal viewpoints differ widely on issues concerning teen pregnancy. However, most share a similar mindset in one regard —*teenagers should definitely not have children.*

The thinking is something like this. Like drinking, smoking, doing drugs, eating disorders, steroid use, and suicide, teen pregnancy is a parent's worst nightmare, indeed a national public health crisis requiring targeted interventions: government-sponsored education sessions, parent meetings, fact sheets, public service announcements, and Web sites. After all, if teen births are associated with unhealthy babies, poverty, welfare, developmental delays, juvenile delinquency, dropping out of school, losing out on a higher education, doing jail time, and an overall bleak future, they must be stopped.

With this perception comes the assumption that teen pregnancies are mostly unintended, resulting from misinformation, teenage irresponsibility, or the teenage mindset of invincibility. After all, what teen would get pregnant on purpose, throwing away her future?

Some statistics do document this theory. According to one study by the National Campaign to Prevent Teen and Unplanned Pregnancy, about eight in ten teen pregnancies *are* unintended, and similarly, about 80 percent of both teens and adults believe that teen pregnancies prevent or delay teen parents from reaching their goals.

However, we are left asking, what about the other 20 percent? One in every five teen girls gets pregnant on purpose? Where is this happening and why?

One small town outside of Boston found itself asking this question when eighteen girls at one high school were discovered to be pregnant, four times the number from the year before. Reports of a "pregnancy pact" soon surfaced—the girls were trying to get pregnant on purpose and raise their babies together.

Furthermore, according to Emily M. White, a resident at Women and Infants' Hospital in Providence, Rhode Island, in some demographic groups the numbers are probably even higher. A study of inner city teen girls reported that 42 percent of girls coming in for their first prenatal visits intentionally did not use birth control. Were these girls uneducated, rebellious, or pressured into sex by their boyfriends? No, none of the above—rather, according to the study, they were "afraid that they would not be able to get pregnant."

While this fear may seem surprising, Kathryn Edin and Maria Kefalas make sense of it in their book *Promises I Can Keep: Why Poor Women Put Motherhood Before Marriage*. During the course of their research, through interviews with and by living among poor women, they came to understand that in these women's world children were viewed as "a necessity, an absolutely essential part of a young woman's life, the chief source of identity and meaning."

In an essay for the *International Journal of Epidemiology*, Janet Rich-Edwards provides another piece of the puzzle when she says, "Where there is no opportunity, there is no cost to early pregnancy." In other words, if college or a career are not on a teen's radar in the first place, having a baby while a teenager would probably not interrupt her dreams. On the other hand, to many poor girls, becoming a mother is "the surest source of accomplishment within their reach," according to Edin and Kefalas.

Other teens, economically disadvantaged and not, *are* reaching for accomplishments and are focused on financial and educational success. Some of them are derailed by unintentional pregnancies; however, others are motivated by them. Thrown into a role of responsibility, they pursue their dreams more steadfastly instead of abandoning them.

Similarly, many pregnant teens without aspirations find themselves getting their act together and planning a future for the sake of their children. In one Australian study a teen mother comments, "I wouldn't change anything because she [the baby] changed my life. I

Teen pregnancy is a complicated issue worthy of serious discussion by today's teens.

was living in [a town] and started to get into drugs really heavily. There was no hope for me and I just see that she saved my life."

There is some research that indicates that this mother is not alone, that babies can motivate teens to find financial success. One study, conducted over several years and cited in a book titled *Kids Having Kids*, compared women from age sixteen to age thirty who had miscarriages to teens who gave birth. By their mid-to-late twenties, moms who had carried their babies to term and were raising them worked more and earned more than their counterparts who had miscarried and did not have children.

Another study, published in the *Journal of Adolescent Health*, reported similar outcomes, finding that mothers giving birth in their teens may attain higher levels of education, employment, and independence in the first five years after the birth of their child. Additionally, teen moms five years out were more satisfied with their partner and sexuality and were generally more satisfied in all other aspects of their lives, with the exception of leisure time and hobbies.

Not all teen pregnancies are accidents or disasters. Some teens find their life's meaning in parenting. Many teens are motivated by their pregnancies to work hard and build a better life for themselves and their children. Other teens do miss out on opportunities and lose sight of educational and career goals in the wake of their pregnancies and have a more difficult life as a direct result of their pregnancies.

Teen pregnancy is an extremely complicated issue and is definitely a matter worthy of discussion by professionals as well as today's students. The articles in this volume represent multiple viewpoints surrounding the issue. In addition, the volume contains two appendixes to help the reader understand and explore the topic, as well as a thorough bibliography and a list of organizations to contact for further information. The appendix titled "What You Should Know About Teen Pregnancy" offers vital facts about pregnancy and how it affects young people. The appendix "What You Should Do About Teen Pregnancy" offers information for young people confronted with this issue. With all these features, *Issues That Concern You: Teen Pregnancy* is an excellent resource on this important topic.

ONE

Teen Pregnancy Is Increasing

Eloise Quintanilla and Uri Friedman

For the first time since the 1990s, teen pregnancy rates have increased. While virtually no one sees this as a good thing, *Christian Science Monitor* contributors Uri Friedman and Eloise Quintanilla (the latter was named a 2008–2009 journalism fellow for National Public Radio) point out in the following article that experts in the fields of education and health care disagree over how to address this trend. Discussions seem to focus on whether safe sex practices or sexual abstinence should be taught, and proponents of each approach seem quick to hold the other responsible for the rise in pregnancies.

A shocking assertion that underage girls promised one another they would become pregnant and raise their babies together has focused a bright light on the resurgent problem of teen pregnancy in America.

Whether there was such a plan in [Gloucester, Massachusetts, an] overwhelmingly white city on Boston's North Shore is in dispute. After Gloucester High School witnessed 17 pregnancies this school year [2007–2008]—more than quadruple last year's average of four—the school principal attributed the surge to a "pact"

City leaders of Gloucester, Massachusetts, meet to discuss issues relating to the alleged pregnancy pact among some Gloucester High School girls.

among "seven or eight" girls in a *Time* magazine article. But at a press conference Monday [June 23, 2008], school Superintendent Christopher Farmer said there was a "distinct possibility" that the girls simply decided post-pregnancy to "come together for mutual support."

Yet the incident is alarming whether or not students entered into a pact, experts say. At a time when the nation's teenage pregnancy rate is rising for the first time since 1991, the Gloucester High controversy has rekindled a longstanding debate over how best to discourage teen pregnancies.

"What's happening in Gloucester is a microcosm in some ways for what we're seeing at the national level," says Bill Albert, chief program officer for the National Campaign to Prevent Teen and Unplanned Pregnancy in Washington. "The good news is that we have made extraordinary progress as a nation [since the early

1990s] in convincing people to delay sexual activity and delay pregnancy and parenthood. The bad news is that that progress seems to have come to a complete standstill and, in some ways, has reversed."

Teen Pregnancy Has Increased

Birthrates for teenagers age 15 to 17 rose by 3 percent between 2005 and 2006, the first increase since 1991, according to preliminary data released in December [2007] by the US Centers for Disease Control and Prevention (CDC). Stephanie Ventura, head of CDC's reproductive statistics branch, says it's too soon to say whether the reversal represents a national trend toward more teen births or is simply a "one-year blip." But she adds that the rapid pace at which teen births declined in the US during the 1990s had grown sluggish in recent years, perhaps setting the stage for the 2006 results.

Another CDC report released [in June 2008] found that condom use among sexually active high school students was essentially unchanged between 2003 and 2007 after steadily increasing from 1991 until 2003. Teen-reported sexual activity rates also underwent no changes between 2005 and 2007.

"There are two things that matter when it comes to preventing pregnancy: not having sex and using contraceptives consistently and carefully," says Mr. Albert. "Both are leveling off at the very best. That may be why we're seeing an increase" in the teen birthrate.

But finding a solution is contentious; there is considerable disagreement over whether educators should emphasize safe sex or abstinence.

Despite spending more than $1 billion since 1996, federal "abstinence until marriage" programs have not taught young people to be sexually responsible, says David Landry of the Guttmacher Institute in New York, a think tank on sexual and reproductive-health issues. A nine-year Mathematica Policy Research study released in 2007 also found that such programs had no effect on teen sexual abstinence.

Birth Rates for Teenagers Aged 15–19 in the United States

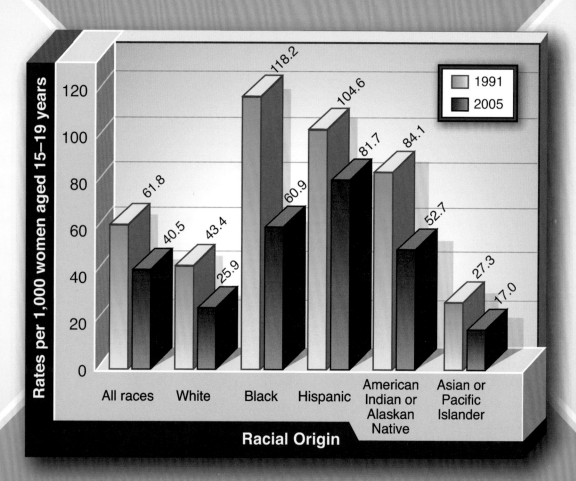

Taken from: Joyce A. Martin et al., "Births: Final Data for 2005," *National Vital Statistics Reports*, vol. 56, no. 6, December 5, 2007. www.cdc.gov/nchs/data/nvsr/nvsr56/nvsr56_06.pdf.

The federal abstinence programs fall short in mandating that instructors mention contraception only in terms of its failure rates, Mr. Landry says. "The misconception of many is that simply talking about using contraception promotes sexual activity."

He supports "comprehensive sexual education," which includes encouraging youth to delay sexual activity and providing medically accurate information about contraception.

Two Sides to the Sexual Education Debate

Yet those who advocate for abstinence education—which teaches teens to abstain from sexual activity—are equally adamant. In an April [2008] report, the Heritage Foundation in Washington detailed 11 studies of abstinence programs that yielded positive findings. The authors censured the government for "spending over $1 billion each year to promote contraception and safe-sex education—at least 12 times what it spends on abstinence education."

The same debates now echo in Gloucester, a blue-collar city with deep Catholic roots. [In May 2008], two officials at Gloucester High's health center resigned in protest because the local hospital refused to distribute contraceptives to students without parental consent. Mayor Carolyn Kirk said . . . the school committee would review a city policy prohibiting the distribution of birth control in schools as it revamps Gloucester's teen-pregnancy policy.

Gloucester Residents Are Also Divided

"As far as birth control pills, they should not be given out at school," says parent Pam Cilluffo, adding that they should be available at home. "Condoms should be distributed at school."

Gloucester graduate Barry Sousa thinks that while more sex education would be beneficial, the problem begins with family dynamics. "My feeling is that these kids don't have a good family life," he says.

Teen pregnancy rates may be surging because officials are diverting resources to social services that seem more pressing, says Albert of the pregnancy-prevention campaign.

Annette Dion, a private music teacher in Gloucester, agrees: "There's plenty of money but [city officials] aren't spending it well."

"There's still an awful lot of questions we need to answer as a community," says Ray Lamont, editor of the *Gloucester Daily Times*. "We are getting bogged down in the details of how to define 'pact' when the real issue is that 17 girls decided to get pregnant. We need to find out why they got pregnant."

TWO

Teen Pregnancy Is Harmful to Society

National Campaign to Prevent Teen Pregnancy and Unplanned Pregnancy

The National Campaign to Prevent Teen Pregnancy and Unplanned Pregnancy is an organization that seeks to ensure that children are born into stable, two-parent families that are committed to and ready for the task of parenthood. Its specific goal is to prevent teen pregnancy and unplanned pregnancy among single, young adults. This article points out the social impact of teen pregnancy, including health issues stemming from less-than-optimal preconception and prenatal care and the poor physical and mental health of children born to teen mothers. It also addresses the impact of poverty, lower educational achievement, and unemployment of single mothers on their children.

A new analysis by the National Campaign to Prevent Teen Pregnancy indicates that about one in three pregnancies in America are unwanted. That is, about one-third—2 million —of the 6.4 million pregnancies in 2001 (the most recent year for which adequate data are available) were unwanted. This figure includes: (1) pregnancies that end in abortion (about 1.3

million); (2) births resulting from pregnancies that women themselves say they did not want at the time of conception or *ever* in the future (about 567,000); and (3) a smaller number of miscarriages that were also from unwanted pregnancies (179,000). This large number of unwanted pregnancies has far-reaching consequences for women, men, children, families, and society. . . .

Reducing unwanted pregnancy will bring significant benefits to women, men, children, families, and society in general. . . .

Unwanted Pregnancies Leave Children Disadvantaged

New guidelines about preconception care from the Centers for Disease Control and Prevention underscore how planning for pregnancy and being at optimal health before pregnancy can help to dramatically improve a woman's chance of having a healthy

Tests show that two-year-old children born of an unwanted pregnancy have significantly lower test scores than children born from a desired pregnancy.

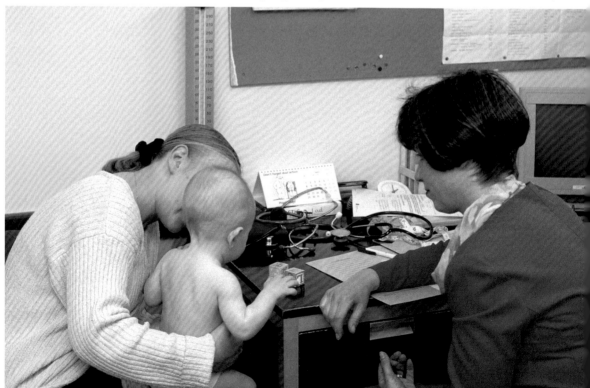

pregnancy and baby. Unfortunately, women who experience an unwanted pregnancy often do not have the opportunity to engage in such preconception care.

Even when taking into account the existing social and economic factors, women experiencing an unwanted pregnancy are less likely to obtain prenatal care and their babies are at increased risk of both low birthweight and of being born prematurely, both of which increase the risk of many serious problems including infant mortality. These mothers are also less likely to breastfeed their infants.

Children born from unwanted pregnancies also face a range of developmental risks as well. For example, these children report poorer physical and mental health compared to those children born as the result of an intended pregnancy. They also have relationships with their mothers that are less close during childhood (and possibly into adulthood) when compared to peers who were born as the result of an intended pregnancy.

A new analysis from Child Trends indicates that, after controlling for numerous background factors, children two years old who were born as the result of an unwanted pregnancy have significantly lower cognitive test scores when compared to children born as the result of an intended pregnancy. These cognitive test scores include direct assessment of such skills as listening, vocabulary, exploring, problem solving, memory, and communication, as well as a child's overall mental ability relative to other children in his or her age group. . . .

Children Benefit from Strong, Welcoming Families

Over two decades of social science research makes clear that children fare better when their parents are older, have completed at least high school, are in stable and committed relationships—marriage, in particular—and are ready to take on the complex challenges of being parents. But many children born as the result of unwanted pregnancies are not welcomed into such families.

The majority of children from an unwanted pregnancy are born to women who are either single or co-habiting. This is important because children who are raised in single-parent families face

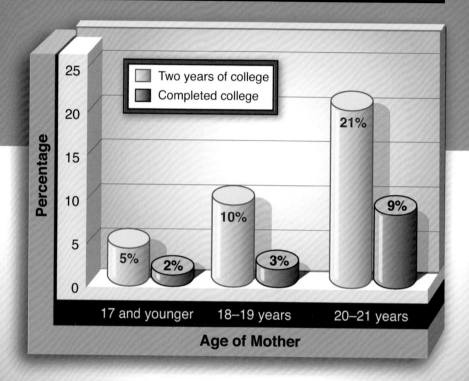

Educational Attainment of Teen Mothers Compared to Mothers Aged 20–21

Two years of college
Completed college

Percentage

- 5% (17 and younger, two years of college)
- 2% (17 and younger, completed college)
- 10% (18–19 years, two years of college)
- 3% (18–19 years, completed college)
- 21% (20–21 years, two years of college)
- 9% (20–21 years, completed college)

17 and younger   18–19 years   20–21 years

Age of Mother

Taken from: Saul D. Hoffman, *By the Numbers: The Public Costs of Teen Childbearing*, October 2006. www.thenationalcampaign.org/costs/pdf/report/6-BTN_Consequences_for_Parents.pdf.

a number of challenges. For example, when compared to similar children who grow up with two parents, children in one-parent families are twice as likely to drop out of high school, 2.5 times as likely to become teen mothers, 1.4 times as likely to be both out of school and out of work, and five times more likely to be poor. Even after adjusting for a variety of relevant social and economic differences, children in single-parent homes have lower grade-point averages, lower college aspirations, and poorer school attendance records. As adults, they also have higher rates of divorce.

Moreover, an analysis of data from 1970 to 1996 by National Campaign President Isabel Sawhill shows that virtually all of the increase in child poverty over that period was related to the growth of single-parent families. In the 1970s, some of this increase was the result of rising divorce rates, but since the early 1980s, virtually all of the increase has been driven by the increased numbers of never-married mothers.

All such data suggest that reducing unwanted pregnancy will increase the proportion of children born into circumstances that better support their growth and development. For example, the National Campaign estimates that preventing unwanted pregnancy has the potential to reduce non-marital child bearing by 26 percent. . . .

Abortions, Poverty, and Education

Although there are many deeply felt and strongly held beliefs nationwide about the proper place of abortion in American life, virtually all of us see value in lessening the need for abortion and would prefer that fewer women have to confront an unwanted pregnancy in the first place. Through primary prevention—that is helping couples avoid unwanted pregnancy—the 1.3 million abortions in America each year can be dramatically decreased.

Disparities in unwanted pregnancy are on the rise. A woman below the poverty line is now nearly four times as likely as a woman at or above 200 percent of poverty to have an unintended pregnancy —a complex measure that includes *both* unwanted and mistimed pregnancy. Reflecting this trend, the abortion rate for low income women increased 22 percent between 1994 and 2000. Still, 40 percent of all unintended pregnancies are to women at or above 200 percent of poverty.

That an unwanted pregnancy can derail the future plans of individuals is self-evident. For example, an unexpected, unwanted pregnancy can interrupt a young person's education and diminish future job prospects—a scenario that is becoming ever more serious with the increasing demand for a well educated workforce. Reducing the high level of unwanted pregnancy in this country will unquestionably help many teens and adults achieve economic security and more stable relationships, which benefits not only them but also their children and society.

THREE

The Difficulties Associated with Teen Pregnancy Also Affect Mothers in Their Twenties

Kelleen Kaye

Writer Kelleen Kaye is a fellow at the New America Foundation and former senior policy analyst for the Department of Health and Human Services (focusing on teen pregnancy and issues related to single parenthood). In the following selection she shows how, while the number of teen pregnancies in recent years has been down, the sociological issues connected with teen parenthood have simply been delayed by a decade. The number of children born to single women is at a record high (with a significant number of these women in their early to mid-twenties), and these women are often unable to continue their education beyond high school, thus finding themselves and their children living at or near poverty levels.

America made teen pregnancy prevention a national priority, and progress on this front is remarkable. However, increasingly, women are avoiding pregnancy as teens, only to become single mothers in their early 20s. Often their entry into parenthood is just as ill-prepared and perilous to child well-being, yet the policy response is far less adequate.

In 1995, President [Bill] Clinton pronounced teen pregnancy an epidemic, and, following his call for action, the National Campaign to Prevent Teen Pregnancy was formed. Congress made teen pregnancy prevention a focus of welfare reform in 1996, and President [George W.] Bush furthered this commitment with policies emphasizing sexual abstinence and family values.

Prevention efforts now extend to both men and women, and to approaches such as media campaigns, mentoring, youth development, and relationship skills. Although the appropriate mix of abstinence, contraception, and other services remains strongly debated, teen childbearing clearly has fallen dramatically since its reduction became a national priority—by 33 percent since 1991—and all efforts likely played some role.

Children Born to Single Mothers Set a Record High

However, society is trading one set of at-risk parents for another. In 2003, more than 1.4 million children were born to single mothers, a record 36 percent. Roughly 40 percent of those births were to single mothers in their early 20s—young adults—and about three-quarters of these young single mothers had only a high school education or less.

Childbearing by singles has grown by over one-quarter since 1990, and young adults account for roughly 60 percent of this increase.

Reducing teen childbearing must remain a national priority, with nearly 415,000 births annually (42 per 1,000 teen women); however, births to young, single adults surpass even "epidemic" levels of teen childbearing, with 550,000 births annually (71 per 1,000 single women ages 20–24).

This new epidemic fails to register as a national priority even though research shows that nearly half the children of single

Childbearing by single mothers has increased 25 percent since 1990, and young adults account for 60 percent of the increase.

mothers live in poverty (four times the rate for children with married parents), and their rates of substance abuse, male incarceration, and teen pregnancy are two to three times greater.

Unmarried, cohabiting mothers do not fare much better. They are twice as likely to break up within five years compared with married mothers, and their children have more than twice the poverty rate, poorer school and behavioral outcomes, and dramatically higher exposure to abuse than children with married parents.

This probably follows from young women's frequently disconnected entry into parenthood. Low-income single mothers portrayed in Kathryn Edin and Maria Kefalas's groundbreaking book, *Promises I Can Keep: Why Poor Women Put Motherhood Before Marriage*, describe many of their pregnancies as neither intended nor prevented. Motherhood is a natural part of their early 20s, a focal point that will bring love and purpose to their lives.

Mothers Need Support

But because they often see the men fathering their children as unfit or even dangerous, they reserve marriage as a lofty goal for later life. Many enter motherhood with high aspirations for their children and a belief that their love will overcome all serious obstacles, but soon replace such hopes with a quest for basic survival, accepting that their children may follow the same paths into single parenthood, drugs, and incarceration, and redefining success to mean loving their children no matter what.

Public policy largely overlooks single childbearing among young adults, citing a lack of programmatic approaches. However, there are clear steps within our grasp. Declining trends in the accessibility of contraceptive services must be reversed. Recently reported findings from the Alan Guttmacher Institute ("Unintended Pregnancies Rise for Poor Women" and "Unintended Pregnancy Linked to State Funding Cuts") indicate that 33 states made it more difficult or more expensive for poor women to obtain contraceptive services between 1994 and 2001, corresponding to a 30 percent increase in unintended pregnancies

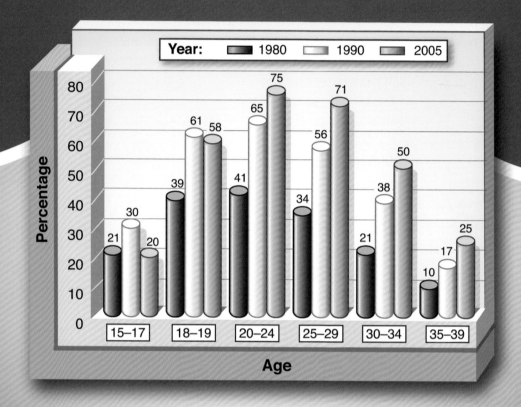

Birth Rates for Unmarried Women by Age in the United States

Year: 1980 ☐ 1990 ☐ 2005

Percentage (y-axis): 0, 10, 20, 30, 40, 50, 60, 70, 80

Age (x-axis):

- 15–17: 21, 30, 20
- 18–19: 39, 61, 58
- 20–24: 41, 65, 75
- 25–29: 34, 56, 71
- 30–34: 21, 38, 50
- 35–39: 10, 17, 25

Taken from: Joyce A. Martin et al., "Births: Final Data for 2005," *National Vital Statistics Reports*, vol. 56, no. 6, December 5, 2007. www.cdc.gov/nchs/data/svsr/nvsr56/nvsr56_06.pdf.

among poor women during the same period. Title X, the only public funding going directly to family-planning clinics, has fallen by two-thirds since 1980.

However, our vision of family planning for young adults must extend beyond simply providing contraceptives. It must address underlying changes in behaviors and attitudes toward parenthood. Innovations are needed that reach young adults effectively, focus on the value of stable, two-parent families and the risks to children raised outside of that structure, and impart a greater sense of responsibility. What's needed most is the same sense of national priority and urgency that accompanied efforts to prevent teen pregnancy.

Without greater attention focused on the pathways into parenthood, society's important efforts to help bring parents into healthy marriages, to help parents support their families through work, and to help keep children from falling through the cracks will continue to be undermined.

FOUR

Poverty Is the Key Factor in Teen Pregnancy

Jonathan Zimmerman

Author Jonathan Zimmerman, who teaches history and education at New York University, contends in this selection that it is poverty that most often results in teens getting pregnant, rather than teen pregnancy leading to poverty (as the issue is usually viewed). Zimmerman points to the failures of both abstinence-only sex education curricula and comprehensive sex education curricula as indicators that the root problem—poverty—has not been addressed. Most teen mothers are already living in poverty, and pregnancy will only perpetuate it. For the few who do not live in poverty, pregnancy will not severely impact their economic or educational opportunities.

One side thinks adolescents should receive more "comprehensive" information about sex, including contraception. The others side favors a more didactic approach, with a simpler message: "abstinence only."

Sound Familiar?

Brace yourself for yet another round in America's perennial teen-pregnancy wars. On Monday [September 1, 2008], GOP [Grand Old Party, i.e., Republican] vice presidential nominee Sarah Palin confirmed that her 17-year-old daughter Bristol is five months pregnant. Faster than you could say "condoms," liberals and conservatives lined up in predictable battle formations. To the liberal camp, of course, the news about Bristol Palin simply confirmed the need for comprehensive sex education in the schools. On the right, meanwhile, Palin's pregnancy spurred new calls for abstinence-only instruction.

They're both wrong.

Neither Approach Seems to Change Teen Behavior

Let's start with conservatives, and their stubborn demand for abstinence-only education. [In 2007], an exhaustive five-year study confirmed that kids receiving this instruction are no more likely to delay sexual intercourse than their peers.

But the abstinence-only sex education program still draws $175 million in federal money and untold sums from states and localities. As governor of Alaska, indeed, Sarah Palin supported abstinence-only education and denounced "explicit sex-ed programs" in the schools.

Yet we still don't have any evidence that these explicit programs work, either. As University of Pennsylvania sociologist Frank Furstenberg confirmed . . . in an exhaustive review of the literature, efforts to prove the effectiveness of comprehensive sex education are "generally unimpressive, to say the least."

We know that these programs can enhance students' knowledge about risky sex behaviors and change their attitudes toward these same behaviors. But can sex education actually influence what kids *do*? As best we can tell, it can't.

There's only one point on which both sides seem to agree: Teen pregnancy is a big problem. They differ on their solutions, of course, but everyone seems to believe that pregnancy hurts the life chances of teenage moms and their children.

Poverty, Not Teen Pregnancy, Causes Social Problems

Again, the data suggest otherwise. As Furstenberg has shown, bearing a child as a teenager doesn't hurt a woman's prospects for education, job advancement or marriage. Ditto for her kids, who don't suffer any measurable consequences from having a teenage mother.

Instead, they suffer for a much more basic reason: They're poor. About two-thirds of teenage mothers live at or below the poverty line at the time they give birth. The less income and opportunity that you have, the more likely you are to become a teenage parent.

About two-thirds of teenage mothers are living below the poverty line at the time they give birth.

So Americans have it exactly backward. Teen pregnancy doesn't deprive our kids of life chances; instead, kids who lack those chances are the ones who get pregnant. Why? Nobody knows for sure. But it seems that young women who have a sense of power and confidence in their lives are more likely to use contraception. Impoverished girls often lack that confidence, so they don't take measures to protect themselves. They are also less likely to have abortions, which are often too expensive or heavily tabooed in poor communities.

And so the war rages, largely untethered by facts. For in the end, this struggle isn't really about facts at all. It's about rival views of sex itself. Left-leaning Americans view sex as a normal part of human development, so they want to give adolescents the information that will help them make responsible decisions about it. But social conservatives think sex should be reserved for one population alone: married people. Everyone else should abstain, especially if they're teenagers.

That helps explain why Sarah Palin—in revealing Bristol's pregnancy—also announced that her daughter will marry Levi Johnston, the 18-year-old father of Bristol's unborn baby. To drive the point home, Johnston has joined the Palins at the GOP convention. It's a family affair, and now he's a part of it.

The decision won immediate acclaim from conservatives, who regard unwedded childbearing as the greatest plague on the land. And there's a significant body of research showing that children raised by two parents do better than those in single-parent homes.

Ignoring the Real Issue

But we also know that so-called "shotgun" marriages—that is, unions forged in response to a pregnancy—are heavily prone to divorce. That's one reason why divorce rates are so much higher in so-called red states, where young people are more likely to marry after conceiving a child.

All things being equal, of course, it's still best for our teenagers—and for their offspring—to delay parenthood. But all things are *not* equal, and that's the whole point here. The hype

Child Well-Being in Rich Countries

Countries are listed in order of their average rank for the six dimensions of child well-being that have been assessed. A light blue background indicates a place in the top third of the table, mid-blue denotes the middle third, and dark blue the bottom third.

Dimensions of child well-being by country	Average ranking position (for all 6 dimensions)	Dimension 1 Material well-being	Dimension 2 Health and safety	Dimension 3 Educational well-being	Dimension 4 Family and peer relationships	Dimension 5 Behaviors and risks	Dimension 6 Subjective well-being
Netherlands	4.2	10	2	6	3	3	1
Sweden	5.0	1	1	5	15	1	7
Denmark	7.2	4	4	8	9	6	12
Finland	7.5	3	3	4	17	7	11
Spain	8.0	12	6	15	8	5	2
Switzerland	8.3	5	9	14	4	12	6
Norway	8.7	2	8	11	10	13	8
Italy	10.0	14	5	20	1	10	10
Ireland	10.2	19	19	7	7	4	5
Belgium	10.7	7	16	1	5	19	16
Germany	11.2	13	11	10	13	11	9
Canada	11.8	6	13	2	18	17	15
Greece	11.8	15	18	16	11	8	3
Poland	12.3	21	15	3	14	2	19
Czech Republic	12.5	11	10	9	19	9	17
France	13.0	9	7	18	12	14	18
Portugal	13.7	16	14	21	2	15	14
Austria	13.8	8	20	19	16	16	4
Hungary	14.5	20	17	13	6	18	13
United States	18.0	17	21	12	20	20	–
United Kingdom	18.2	18	12	17	21	21	20

Taken from: *UNICEF, Child Poverty in Perspective: An Overview of Child Well-Being in Rich Countries,* Innocenti Report Card 7. UNICEF Innocenti Research Centre, Florence, 2007. http://unicef-icdc.org/publications/pdf/rc7_eng.pdf.

over teen pregnancy diverts us from the truly serious problem in American society, which is the growing poverty of teenagers themselves. [In 2007], for example, UNICEF [United Nations Children's Fund] ranked the United States second to last among 21 developed Western nations in child health, safety and material well-being. Changing the teen pregnancy rate won't change any of that.

So don't feel sorry for Bristol Palin or her unborn child, who will probably turn out OK. So did Ann Dunham, who bore a son when she was just 18. You've probably heard of him: Barack Obama. He seems to have done pretty well, too.

Instead, think about the teen parents who lack the social and material advantages that you do. Remember that in most cases they're parents because they're poor, and not the other way around. The more we fight about teen pregnancy, the less we'll focus upon teen poverty. And that's bad news for all of us.

FIVE

Celebrity Pregnancies Encourage Teen Pregnancy

Nancy Redd

Nancy Redd, author of *The New York Times* best seller *Body Drama* and contributing editor for *CosmoGirl!*, suggests in the following article that pregnant celebrities influence teen girls to get pregnant purposefully. Media portrayal of expectant celebrities glamorizes pregnancy for many teens, while the toll that pregnancy takes on the body as well as the difficulties in raising children are downplayed. Teen girls may also use pregnancy as a means to elicit assurance of affection from their boyfriends, and they may even come to see the birth of a child as a guarantee of unconditional love from someone.

An "it" bag. Designer shoes. A hot boyfriend. Those are usually the must-have accessories in Hollywood. But lately, it seems as though a baby bump is the new status symbol to flaunt. "Bump watches" and detailed news of stars' pregnancies are driving tabloid sales (think Ashlee Simpson, Nicole Richie, Angelina Jolie, and Jessica Alba). A pregnant teen was depicted as a likeable lead character in the Oscar-winning movie *Juno*. And gossip blogs discuss the every move of Jamie Lynn Spears, who

Some people maintain that celebrity pregnancies, such as Angelina Jolie's, are giving teenagers the misguided idea that pregnancy is cool.

got pregnant at 16. It's one thing for teen pregnancies to be popular in Hollywood; what's troubling is that the trend seems to be trickling down to real life. When I interviewed girls about their body issues for my book, *Body Drama*, I was surprised by their nonchalant attitude about teenage pregnancy. When I was in high school it was a taboo, but today, it seems like not that big of a deal—and even somehow cool. One girl said to me, "We all know at least one girl who's a teen mom, and all my friends have thought about what it would be like to have a baby. It doesn't seem that hard." For the first time in more than a decade, the number of teenage pregnancies is rising. Nearly 1 out of every 24 girls ages 15 to 19—that's more than 435,000—are likely to give birth this year [2008]. And statistics suggest that over 10 percent of those pregnancies are on purpose. It used to be thought that planned teen pregnancy was an issue only for lower-income girls who stood to gain welfare benefits and "stay in the system" if they had a baby. But the truth is more complicated. More teens—from all economic classes and backgrounds—are trying to get pregnant. Could there be a connection between our celebrity baby obsession and the extra 10,000 teen pregnancies the United States may see this year?

Baby Fever

Experts say yes. "Teens see how glamorous pregnant celebrities are made out to be, and how much attention they and their babies are getting, and some girls start to think a baby will bring similar results to them," says Dyan Aretakis, director of the University of Virginia Teen Health Center. Even stars may not be immune to the hype. When Jamie Lynn Spears's pregnancy was announced, her aunt, Chanda McGovern, speculated whether it was on purpose, saying that Jamie Lynn was "wanting a little 'me' attention because of everything that's going on with Britney."

When we see our idols on TV and in magazines, we covet their clothes, their houses, and their lifestyles. It seems stars have enough influence to make some of us want to emulate their pregnancies too. Lisa Oldham, M.D., an ob-gyn in Chicago who sees many pregnant teens, agrees that celebs have a lot of influence. "Jamie Lynn Spears can afford to get pregnant without the same hardship of typical teens," she says. "(Seeing how easy her pregnancy looks) may encourage a teen who looks up to her to think, Well, if she can do it, why can't I?" Just think of all the photos we see of celeb kids, like Suri Cruise and the Jolie-Pitt clan. They are rarely pictured crying and often are shown wearing designer clothes while at birthday parties or shopping for toys. Their family life seems so fun and glamorous. But most teen girls don't have a celebrity's cash flow or multiple live-in nannies to help take care of their babies.

The Fantasy Does Not Succeed Outside of Hollywood

It's this illusion of a fairy-tale family life that may be what's driving more teens than ever to get pregnant on purpose. "The three biggest reasons I see behind purposeful teenage pregnancies are to get their guy to stay, to have someone to love them unconditionally, and to create a purpose in their lives," says Hatim Omar, M.D., director of the Adolescent Medicine and Young Parent Program at the University of Kentucky in Lexington. "It's easy to think that having a baby will help keep your boyfriend attached to you for life," adds Aretakis. "Unfortunately, what happens with most of my patients is that the guys eventually abandon their girlfriends and their babies, financially and emotionally." Rachel, 18, from Farmington, Utah—who intentionally became pregnant at 17—can relate. "My boyfriend and I were off and on, and I decided to secretly get pregnant to make him be with me full-time," says Rachel, who comes from an upper-middle-class background. "I told him that he didn't have to use condoms because I could only get pregnant at a certain time of each month, even though I knew that wasn't true." When Rachel became pregnant, she was relieved. "I got what I wanted—his mom made him propose, and we set a wedding date and ordered invitations. But after a while, I realized he wasn't right for me and called off the wedding." Sadly, after all she'd been through, Rachel lost her baby shortly before giving birth.

Elizabeth, 23, from New York City, met her baby's father when she was 19 and quickly became pregnant with her son, now 3. "I thought it would be cool to have a baby," she says. "I thought, He's going to love me forever." Dr. Omar says some of the 600-plus teen moms he sees each year tried to become pregnant because, like Elizabeth, "they were desperate for attention and unconditional love." This isn't unusual, says Wendy Hart Beckman, author of *Dating, Relationships, and Sexuality: What Teens Should Know.* "When I taught a high school class, some girls got pregnant because they weren't sure if their boyfriends truly loved them, but they knew they could be certain of the love of a baby."

Angela Diaz, M.D., director of the Mount Sinai Adolescent Center in New York City, believes that many teen pregnancies stem from feelings of hopelessness about the future or loneliness. "When they're depressed or suffering from low self-esteem, some girls imagine motherhood as a way to feel a purpose in their lives," she says. Especially in communities where there are a lot of young mothers, it's almost encouraged. At the very least, no one raises an eyebrow. Scott Kizner, Ph.D., school superintendent in Martinsville, Virginia, where the teen pregnancy rate is one of the highest in the state, agrees. "If a goal like college doesn't seem achievable or interesting, and if there are no positive role models around, it's hard for some girls to imagine a future more satisfying than being a mother," he says. "Especially when their friends bring their babies to school like a trophy, and they're fussed over like they're celebrities."

Pregnant teenagers seem to be in vogue.

The Reality Looks Bleak for Teen Mothers

Sure, there are communities where teen pregnancy isn't out of the ordinary, and high schools where it's normal for teen moms to bring their babies to class. But the truth is that in our mainstream culture, there's still a social stigma surrounding having a baby when you're a teenager. And the statistics on how much harder it is to get ahead as a teen with a baby are startling: Eighty percent of teen moms end up as single moms. Over 60 percent of

The Not-So-Glamorous Side of Teen Pregnancy

The children of teenaged mothers are more likely to:

- Score lower in math and reading into adolescence.

- Repeat a school grade.

- Be in poor health (as reported by the mother).

- Be taken to emergency rooms for care as infants.

- Be victims of abuse and neglect.

- Be placed in foster care and spend more time in foster care.

- Be incarcerated at some point during adolescence or their early twenties.

- Drop out of high school, give birth as a teenager, or be unemployed or underemployed as a young adult.

Taken from: Centers for Disease Control and Prevention, "Teen Pregnancy."
www.cdc.gov/reproductivehealth/AdolescentReproHealth/PDF/TeenPreg-FS.pdf.

teenage mothers never complete high school, and as a result, they tend to be more depressed and earn less money in adulthood—hundreds of thousands of dollars less over a lifetime than women who waited to have kids. Only 1.5 percent of teenage moms earn a college degree before the age of 30. Plus, nearly 80 percent of children born to single teen mothers drop out of high school and end up living in poverty themselves, compared to only 9 percent of children born to married women with high school diplomas.

"It's harder as a teenage mother to reach your goals," says Dr. Diaz. "You're no longer making decisions just for yourself and your needs, which makes it difficult to excel." Not only did Elizabeth, the mother of the 3-year-old, find her baby demanding of her time, but her boyfriend was also a big burden, insisting that she drop out of school to take care of their son. That threw a wrench into her career and financial plans. Rachel, from the upper-middle-class neighborhood in Utah, didn't have to worry about financially taking care of her baby. Her mom, who was initially devastated by the news of her pregnancy, agreed to help with money. But even though her financial future looked more promising than Elizabeth's, Rachel soon realized that her pregnancy wasn't the joyful event she'd hoped for. "When people found out I was pregnant, I was immediately labeled a bad person by my entire extended family," she says. "Nothing hurt as much as my 6-year-old stepsister telling me I was no longer her role model." Since losing her baby, Rachel has enrolled in college and feels "like I've gotten a second chance."

The Future Depends on Real Conversations

No one can deny that it's a troubling phenomenon: Girls too young to vote, drink, and even drive are having babies. But what do we do about it? For starters, instead of gossiping about the Jamie Lynns of the world, we as a society need to start discussing the unglamorous realities of teen pregnancy. "If I knew then what I know now about what pregnancy does to your body, I would have done things a lot differently," says Rachel. Sure, airbrushed pictures in magazines make new moms appear glamorous and glowing, but the reality is anything but—stretch marks, swollen and leaky breasts, extra weight (teen moms are at a much higher risk for eventual obesity than women who wait to have kids), and incontinence (the inability to hold in your urine) are just some of the unattractive side effects of a postpregnancy body. And unlike a handbag or even a boyfriend, your body can't be traded in for a more stylish or attractive version.

It's okay to dream about having what celebs have, but it should end at designer shoes or clothes. Having a baby is a beautiful thing, but having one too soon, even if you think you're ready, can become more of a night-mare than a dream come true. When I was in high school, a friend of mine got pregnant so her boyfriend would stay with her. It didn't work—after they had two kids together, he ended up cheating on her and they broke up. I always thought she was smarter than I was, but she was never able to finish college. Nine years later, she still lives in her parents' house with her children and works at her high school fast-food job, a far cry from her dream of teaching and traveling the world. When I go home and see her, it makes me sad to think of all she could have accomplished if she had made different choices. But my hope is that the more you know about what really happens if you get pregnant in your teens, the less likely you'll be to allow yourself to make that mistake. Take it from someone who knows: "I love my son, but I could have given him a better life if I'd gone to college first," says Elizabeth. "I wish I would have waited."

SIX

Evangelical Teens Are More Likely to Become Pregnant

Margaret Talbot

While teens' attitudes toward sex are greatly influenced by religious beliefs, sexual behavior is not so influenced —so contends Margaret Talbot, staff writer for *The New Yorker* and senior fellow at the New America Foundation, in the following viewpoint. Evangelical teens tend to become sexually active earlier than their peers and are significantly more likely to engage in unprotected sex. And, while premarital sex is looked down upon in Evangelical circles, teen pregnancy does not seem to cause much shock or bring about shunning. However, among Evangelical youth who are strong adherents to their faith, there is a significantly lower amount of sexual activity and pregnancy.

I n early September [2008], when Sarah Palin, the Republican candidate for Vice-President, announced that her unwed seventeen-year-old daughter, Bristol, was pregnant, many liberals were shocked, not by the revelation but by the reaction to it. They expected the news to dismay the evangelical voters that John McCain was courting with his choice of Palin. Yet reports from the floor of the Republican Convention, in St. Paul, quoted dozens of delegates who seemed unfazed, or even buoyed, by the news. A delegate from Louisiana told CBS News, "Like so many other American families who are in the same situation, I think it's great that she instilled in her daughter the values to have the child and not to sneak off someplace and have an abortion." A Mississippi delegate claimed that "even though young children are making that decision to become pregnant, they've also decided to take responsibility for their actions and decided to follow up with that and get married and raise this child." Palin's family drama, delegates said, was similar to the experience of many socially conservative Christian families. As Marlys Popma, the head of evangelical outreach for the McCain campaign, told *National Review*, "There hasn't been one evangelical family that hasn't gone through some sort of situation." In fact, it was Popma's own "crisis pregnancy" that had brought her into the movement in the first place.

During the campaign, the media has largely respected calls to treat Bristol Palin's pregnancy as a private matter. But the reactions to it have exposed a cultural rift that mirrors America's dominant political divide. Social liberals in the country's "blue states" tend to support sex education and are not particularly troubled by the idea that many teen-agers have sex before marriage, but would regard a teen-age daughter's pregnancy as devastating news. And the social conservatives in "red states" generally advocate abstinence-only education and denounce sex before marriage, but are relatively unruffled if a teen-ager becomes pregnant, as long as she doesn't choose to have an abortion.

Religion and Sexual Behavior

A handful of social scientists and family-law scholars have recently begun looking closely at this split. [In 2007], Mark Regnerus, a sociologist at the University of Texas at Austin, published a startling book called *Forbidden Fruit: Sex and Religion in the Lives of American Teenagers*, and he is working on a follow-up that includes a section titled "Red Sex, Blue Sex." His findings are

Evangelical students march on San Francisco's city hall to promote their views on abstinence from sex until marriage.

drawn from a national survey that Regnerus and his colleagues conducted of some thirty-four hundred thirteen-to-seventeen-year-olds, and from a comprehensive government study of adolescent health known as Add Health. Regnerus argues that religion is a good indicator of attitudes toward sex, but a poor one of sexual behavior, and that this gap is especially wide among teenagers who identify themselves as evangelical. The vast majority of white evangelical adolescents—seventy-four per cent—say that they believe in abstaining from sex before marriage. (Only half of mainline Protestants, and a quarter of Jews, say that they believe in abstinence.) Moreover, among the major religious groups, evangelical virgins are the least likely to anticipate that sex will be pleasurable, and the most likely to believe that having sex will cause their partners to lose respect for them. (Jews most often cite pleasure as a reason to have sex, and say that an unplanned pregnancy would be an embarrassment.) But, according to Add Health data, evangelical teen-agers are more sexually active than Mormons, mainline Protestants, and Jews. On average, white evangelical Protestants make their "sexual début"—to use the festive term of social-science researchers—shortly after turning sixteen. Among major religious groups, only black Protestants begin having sex earlier.

Another key difference in behavior, Regnerus reports, is that evangelical Protestant teen-agers are significantly less likely than other groups to use contraception. This could be because evangelicals are also among the most likely to believe that using contraception will send the message that they are looking for sex. It could also be because many evangelicals are steeped in the abstinence movement's warnings that condoms won't actually protect them from pregnancy or venereal disease. More provocatively, Regnerus found that only half of sexually active teen-agers who say that they seek guidance from God or the Scriptures when making a tough decision report using contraception every time. By contrast, sixty-nine per cent of sexually active youth who say that they most often follow the counsel of a parent or another trusted adult consistently use protection.

Abstinence Pledges May Delay but Do Not Prevent Premarital Sex

The gulf between sexual belief and sexual behavior becomes apparent, too, when you look at the outcomes of abstinence-pledge movements. Nationwide, according to a 2001 estimate, some two and a half million people have taken a pledge to remain celibate

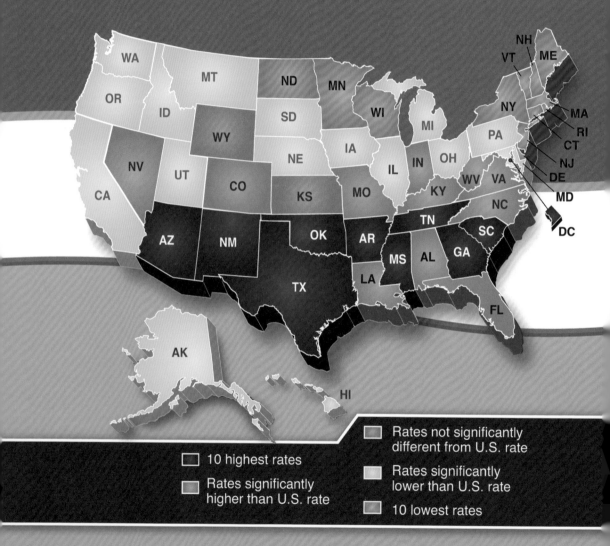

Birth Rates for Teenagers Aged 15–19 Years by State, 2005

WA
MT
ND
MN
OR
ID
WY
SD
WI
MI
NH
VT
ME
NY
MA
RI
CT
NJ
DE
MD
PA
NV
UT
CO
NE
IA
IL
IN
OH
WV
VA
CA
KS
MO
KY
NC
TN
SC
AZ
NM
OK
AR
MS
AL
GA
DC
LA
TX
FL
AK
HI

10 highest rates

Rates significantly higher than U.S. rate

Rates not significantly different from U.S. rate

Rates significantly lower than U.S. rate

10 lowest rates

Taken from: Joyce A. Martin et al., "Births: Final Data for 2005." *National Vital Statistics Reports*, vol. 56, no. 6, December 5, 2007. www.cdc.gov/nchs/data/nvsr/nvsr56/nvsr56_06.pdf.

until marriage. Usually, they do so under the auspices of movements such as True Love Waits or the Silver Ring Thing. Sometimes, they make their vows at big rallies featuring Christian pop stars and laser light shows, or at purity balls, where girls in frothy dresses exchange rings with their fathers, who vow to help them remain virgins until the day they marry. More than half of those who take such pledges—which, unlike abstinence-only classes in public schools, are explicitly Christian—end up having sex before marriage, and not usually with their future spouse. The movement is not the complete washout its critics portray it as: pledgers delay sex eighteen months longer than non-pledgers, and have fewer partners. Yet, according to the sociologists Peter Bearman, of Columbia University, and Hannah Brückner, of Yale, communities with high rates of pledging also have high rates of S.T.D.s [sexually transmitted diseases]. This could be because more teens pledge in communities where they perceive more danger from sex (in which case the pledge is doing some good); or it could be because fewer people in these communities use condoms when they break the pledge.

Bearman and Brückner have also identified a peculiar dilemma: in some schools, if too many teens pledge, the effort basically collapses. Pledgers apparently gather strength from the sense that they are an embattled minority; once their numbers exceed thirty per cent, and proclaimed chastity becomes the norm, that special identity is lost. With such a fragile formula, it's hard to imagine how educators can ever get it right: once the self-proclaimed virgin clique hits the thirty-one-per-cent mark, suddenly it's Sodom and Gomorrah.

Strong Communities May Prevent Premarital Sex

Religious belief apparently does make a potent difference in behavior for one group of evangelical teen-agers: those who score highest on measures of religiosity—such as how often they go to church, or how often they pray at home. But many Americans who identify themselves as evangelicals, and who hold socially conservative beliefs, aren't deeply observant.

Even more important than religious conviction, Regnerus argues, is how "embedded" a teen-ager is in a network of friends, family, and institutions that reinforce his or her goal of delaying sex, and that offer a plausible alternative to America's sexed-up consumer culture. A church, of course, isn't the only way to provide a cohesive sense of community. Close-knit families make a difference. Teen-agers who live with both biological parents are more likely to be virgins than those who do not. And adolescents who say that their families understand them, pay attention to their concerns, and have fun with them are more likely to delay intercourse, regardless of religiosity.

SEVEN

Evangelical Teens Are Not More Likely to Become Pregnant

Michael Gerson

Evangelical teens are not more likely to be sexually active or to become pregnant than other teens, suggests *Washington Post* columnist and *Newsweek* contributor Michael Gerson in the following viewpoint. Sexually speaking, Evangelical teens are average. Gerson does not believe that sex education curricula, sexual abstinence talks, or sermonizing will be effective in stemming the tide of teen pregnancies. Rather, developing strong communities that foster hope and positive self-image in young people, as well as maintaining high expectations among teens, are presented as the answer.

Recent books and studies seem to indicate disturbing sexual trends among evangelical Christians. And this time we're not talking about their pastors or political leaders. The new attention is on evangelical teenagers, who reportedly start sex earlier than their mainline Protestant peers.

One gleeful headline on an Internet site recently read: "Evangelical Girls Are Easy." That is not the way I remember it.

Now, in the cruel march of years, I have a child on the verge of joining the tribe of the teenager, and its rituals hold sudden

Opinions About Religious Influence on Teen Pregnancy

Teens and adults were asked whether they agreed or disagreed with the following statement: Religious leaders and groups should be doing more to help prevent teen pregnancy.

At least two conclusions have been drawn from these findings. First, it is clear that most young people make decisions about sex based not just on what is safe but also on what they believe is right. Second, there is a real opportunity for religious leaders and faith communities to do more to help young people on this front—based on the strong support of adults and the growing interest of teens.

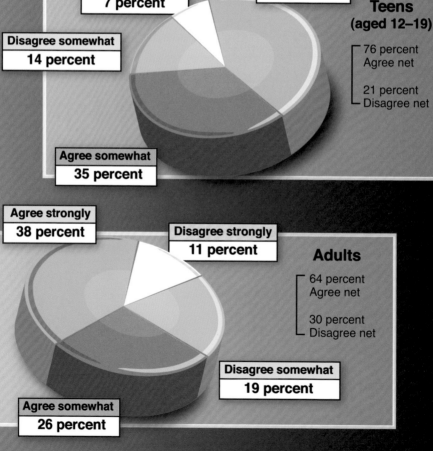

Disagree strongly
7 percent

Agree strongly
41 percent

Teens
(aged 12–19)

┌ 76 percent
  Agree net

  21 percent
└ Disagree net

Disagree somewhat
14 percent

Agree somewhat
35 percent

Agree strongly
38 percent

Disagree strongly
11 percent

Adults

┌ 64 percent
  Agree net

  30 percent
└ Disagree net

Disagree somewhat
19 percent

Agree somewhat
26 percent

Taken from: Bill Albert, *With One Voice 2007: America's Adults and Teens Sound Off About Teen Pregnancy: A Periodic National Survey*, February 2007. Copyright 2007 by the National Campaign to Prevent Teen Pregnancy. www.thenationalcampaign.org/resources/pdf/pubs/WOV2007_fulltext.pdf.

interest. In this circumstance, a parent has a choice between turning to sociology or turning to drink. So I called a bright young sociologist at the University of Virginia named W. Bradford Wilcox in search of consolation.

Wilcox argues, in a paper for the Russell Sage Foundation, that the facts are more complicated and more hopeful than the sniggering media caricature.

Protestant Teens Are Actually Average

When the statistics on teen sexuality are controlled for social and economic factors, conservative Protestant teens first have sex at about the same time as their peers—the average is midway through their 16th year. That is hardly comforting to conservative Protestant parents, who would expect more bang for the bucks they spend funding Sunday schools—well, actually, less bang.

But these numbers shift when controlled for religious intensity. For those who attend church often, sexual activity is delayed until nearly 17, while nominal evangelicals begin at 16.2 years, earlier than the national average.

This trend is more pronounced in other measures of sexual behavior. Only 1 percent of conservative Protestants who attend church weekly cohabit, compared with 10 percent of all adults. (On this statistic, nominal evangelicals almost exactly mirror the nation.) Twelve percent of churchgoing evangelicals have children out of wedlock, compared with 33 percent of all mothers.

These facts, according to Wilcox, support some liberal claims and some conservative ones. Liberals are correct that economic and cultural factors matter greatly, sometimes more than individual belief. Teens with good life prospects and a strong sense of the future—kids with economic and educational ambitions—tend to avoid risky behavior such as drugs and early sex. Without those prospects, the temptation to live for the moment is strong.

Community Is Important

The facts also support a basic conservative belief: that it is difficult for teens to be moral alone. Wilcox argues that teen sexual behavior *can* be influenced—that teenagers can be more than the sum of their hormones. But responsible behavior requires both "norms" and "networks." An intellectual belief in right and wrong is not sufficient. Teens require a community that supports their good choices, especially in times of testing and personal crisis. "Kids who are embedded in a social network with shared norms," he concludes, "are more likely to abide by them."

Sociologist Peter Berger calls these networks "plausibility structures"—sources of authority that do more than lecture or shame; they define the meaning of common sense. When institutions such as religious groups, families, government and the

An instructor teaches an abstinence class in Birmingham, Alabama. The school received a grant from the New Hope Baptist Church to fund the class.

media send a strong and consistent message—smoking is stupid, driving under the influence is criminal, teen pregnancy is self-destructive—we have sometimes seen dramatic changes in behavior. Teen pregnancy and birth rates in the United States, for example, have declined by about one-third since the early 1990s.

The Left Has Communities of Influence, Too

These messages of responsibility are often reinforced by tightknit religious communities, but they are not owned by them. Wilcox notes that American liberal elites often "talk left and walk right, living disciplined lives and expecting their children to do the same, even when they hold liberal social views." Divorce rates among college-educated Americans, he points out, have fallen since the 1980s, as it became more evident that casual divorce did not serve the long-term interests of their children.

The decisive role of authoritative communities in determining individual behavior should not surprise conservatives. Conservatism teaches that individuals are not inherently good and so must be carefully civilized. They need social structures and networks that foster duty and discipline and define those commitments as common sense. In *The Quest for Community*, Robert Nisbet warned: "Release man from the contexts of community and you get not freedom and rights but intolerable aloneness and subjection to demoniac fears and passions."

It would be nice if teen sexual behavior could be automatically changed by an abstinence lecture or a sermon. Setting those norms and expectations, however, is a small part of a larger cultural task. Moral men and women need moral communities.

EIGHT

Positive Male Role Models for Boys Will Decrease Teen Pregnancy

Bob Ray Sanders

Fort Worth (TX) Star-Telegram columnist Bob Ray Sanders reports in the following article that one way to address the issue of teen pregnancy is to confront teen boys on the subject. Manhood must be seen as stepping up to responsibilities, rather than being able to procreate. Girls should not allow themselves to be played against one another for the affections of a boy; they should demand the respect they deserve. Solid sex education is needed early on, since girls are getting pregnant as early as age eleven. Also needed are positive role models for young men— mentors who will help instill a sense of true manhood.

A fter publication of a recent column that mentioned Republican vice-presidential nominee Sarah Palin's unwed 17-year-old pregnant daughter, I heard from several people upset that I would dare mention the child or the family's "private matter."

Some experts say that having a positive role model can help teen boys take more responsibility in their relationships.

There were those people, however, angry not because I brought up the subject of teenage pregnancy, but because I never mentioned the boy who had fathered the child.

"Nobody ever talks about the boys," one reader wrote. "Girls don't get pregnant all by themselves."

Let me say up front that I don't cut males any slack for their role in producing the hundreds of thousands of babies born to teenage girls in this country every year.

For years I have been one who talks to (and about) young boys and men who don't take responsibility for their actions, including engaging in out-of-wedlock and unprotected sex.

For several years I made annual appearances at one Dallas high school, which had a very high teen-pregnancy rate, to hold an assembly with boys only. With the principal observing, we had frank—sometimes heated—discussions about sexual activity, respect for females and themselves, and about simply being accountable for their own deeds.

True Fatherhood

I'll never forget that during one of those sessions, an arrogant young man stood up, proudly announced that he had fathered a child, and basically dared me to say anything about it.

"I have just one question for you," I told him. "Since you are a father, are you taking care of your baby?"

"My mother sends her money every week," he proclaimed.

"Your mother is sending money?" I asked. "Your mother, who I am sure is working hard to take care of you, now has to take care of your child?"

"Yeah," he said, to the jeers of his fellow classmates.

"Let me just suggest that you indeed sired a child. But you are no father."

Most of the other boys applauded.

After the assembly, that student and two other young dads came to me and talked privately about responsibility and the peer pressures they had in their macho world in which it was considered admirable to get a girl pregnant but not so cool to be seen taking care of a baby.

Girls Should Stick Up for Themselves

Then there was a time when I made regular visits to the school for pregnant girls in Fort Worth. On one of my visits, I arrived just as staff members were breaking up a fight between two girls that took place right in front of the principal's office.

When I learned what the girls had been fighting about, I begged the principal to let them come to the assembly. In referencing the fight, which all the students were aware of, I told them why the girls had been battling: They were both pregnant by the same 22-year-old man.

I told the group, "Instead of them fighting each other, they should have been teaming up to go after his sorry behind."

The girls in the room cheered.

A couple of weeks later, in preparing a story on teenage pregnancy for public television, I got a chance to meet the young man at the home of one of the girls—the one he said he truly loved and planned to marry after she graduated from school.

He had been in the military, he said, and he had not planned to get anyone pregnant, much less two girls.

"It was something that just happened," he said.

When I told him I had called him "sorry" in front of a bunch of girls, he said that he could understand why some people might feel that way but that he hoped one day to prove me wrong.

We Need More Sex Education

There is nothing more sobering than standing in a room looking out at the faces and the bellies of 300 or so pregnant teenagers.

You can't do that without feeling for each of them, and without thinking about the lack of responsibility of males.

We have got to talk to our children about sex. And, yes, we need sex education in our schools, starting in elementary. School officials once told me of an 11-year-old student who was pregnant.

Parenting, of course, is important, but good parenting is no guarantee that kids won't get in trouble.

Children of some of the best parents in the world still make grave mistakes that will affect them for the rest of their lives.

Males Who Witnessed Violence Against Their Mothers Are More Likely to Impregnate Teenage Girls

Type and Frequency of Battery	Sample Size (number)	Impregnated Teenage Girl (percent)
Mother was pushed, grabbed, slapped or thrown at		
Never	3,294	17.9
Once or twice	435	18.9
Sometimes	307	24.8
Often or very often	91	35.2
Kicked, bitten, hit with fist, hit with something hard		
Never	3,727	18.1
Once or twice	175	21.7
Sometimes	175	28.0
Often or very often	50	40.0
Hit repeatedly over at least a few minutes		
Never	3,899	18.1
Once or twice	102	35.3
Sometimes	95	25.3
Often or very often	31	45.2
Threatened with a knife or gun or had a knife or gun used to hurt her		
Never	4,047	18.7
Once or twice	60	30.0
Sometimes	14	35.7
Often or very often	6	33.3

Taken from: Robert F. Anda et al., "Abused Boys, Battered Mothers, and Male Involvement in Teen Pregnancy," *Pediatrics*, vol. 107, no. 2, February 2001. http://pediatrics.aappublications.org/cgi/reprint/107/2/e19.

As the father of a son, and a man who has scores of nephews, I know that boys and young men look for guidance on tough, sometimes personal issues even when they act like they don't want or appreciate it.

One of the best ways we can educate them is through example.

Boys need positive male role models in their lives, and it's incumbent on us to be there for them—not just for our own, but also for those who happen to be somebody else's children.

NINE

Adult Men Cause Most Teen Pregnancies

Hayley Graham

While many people assume that most pregnant teen girls have been sexually active with teen boys, information from the National Campaign to Prevent Teen and Unplanned Pregnancy suggests that there is a larger age gap between the pregnant girls and their sex partners, with the majority of girls becoming pregnant by men a number of years older than them. Writer Hayley Graham, a reporter for *The Kankakee (IL) Daily Journal*, points out in this selection not only the legal repercussions of these sexual relationships, but also the issues of emotional and physical safety for young women in relationships with older men, as there is a significantly greater risk of abuse.

Teenage mother Kortesha Jones's story is a familiar one. She's part of a growing national epidemic fueled by insufficient sex education, the sexualization of young women in the media and ignorance.

Two stories have brought this issue front and center in the public discourse: The recent high-profile teenage pregnancy of Alaskan [governor] Sarah Palin's daughter, and her engagement

Hayley Graham, "Most Teen Pregnancies Caused by Adult Men," *Daily Journal*, October 13, 2008. Reproduced by permission.

to her teenage boyfriend, as well as the recent hit movie, *Juno*, which portrayed teen pregnancy as humorous and whimsical.

But both images do not give an accurate picture of the problem or those involved.

Half of the time, a teen pregnancy does not even involve two teens close in age. The National Campaign to Prevent Teen and Unplanned Pregnancy estimates 52 percent of the fathers are three years or more older than the moms; and about two-thirds of the fathers are age 20 and over.

In Illinois, the largest group of fathers involved in fathering a child with a teenage mother were between the ages of 20 and 24—that age group accounted for 48 percent of teen births during 2006, the latest year available. Only 10 percent of the fathers were under age 18.

"There is reason for parents to be concerned with these types of relationships," said Bill Albert, chief program officer for the National Campaign to Prevent Teen and Unplanned Pregnancy.

In 2006, 48 percent of teen births in Illinois were fathered by men between twenty and twenty-four years old.

Abusive Roles

The older the partner, the greater the risk for abuse.

One in five American teen girls has had sex with a sexual part-ner who is three or more years older, according to a report released in April [2008] by Child Trends, an independent research center that focuses on children and families.

Even if the relationship is consensual, there is a significant power difference that puts the man in a controlling role.

The risk of unplanned pregnancy and sexually transmitted dis-ease increases significantly with older partners because they are less likely to use condoms, the report said.

Kortesha started having sex with her then boyfriend last sum-mer, but the two used condoms only occasionally. Her mother, Teresa Carroll, said she talked to her daughter about the effec-tiveness of condoms, but Kortesha said using protection did not always seem necessary and emotions often took over.

These relationships are still considered a form of sex abuse whether they are consensual or not, and many occur with a teenag-er who has had a history of previous abuse. (There is no indica-tion that this is the case with Kortesha.)

Darkness to Light, an international non-profit [organization] that raises awareness of sex abuse, estimates 60 percent of teens' first pregnancies are preceded by molestation, rape or attempted rape.

"We ignore the fact that many of these young women are groomed into being sexually abused and are victims of a crime," said Pat Patrick, vice president of Darkness to Light. "These are still children being victimized."

A number of studies have indicated a strong correlation between the abuse and teen pregnancy, according to Patrick. When children are sexualized at a young age, and that barrier is broken, they become more promiscuous.

Criminal Fatherhoods

Kankakee [Illinois] Detective [Sergeant] Jay Etzel said most cases like Kortesha's go unreported. The handful that are reported often do not get prosecuted.

Do you think it is okay for teens to be in a relationship with someone three or more years older?

Research shows that relationships between those aged twelve to fourteen and a partner who is older by two, three, or more years—compared to relationships with someone only slightly older, the same age, or younger—are much more likely to include sexual intercourse. For example 13 percent of same-age relationships among those aged twelve to fourteen include sexual intercourse. If the partner is two years older, 26 percent of the relationships include sex. If the partner is three or more years older, 33 percent of the relationships include sex.

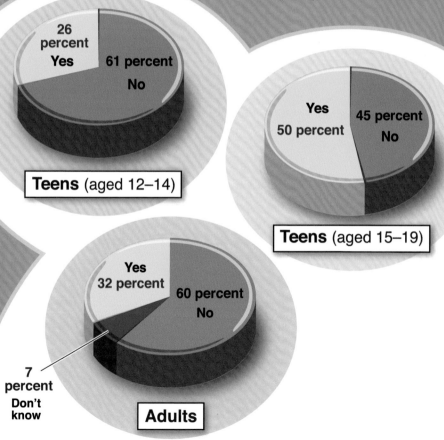

Teens (aged 12–14)
- 26 percent Yes
- 61 percent No

Teens (aged 15–19)
- Yes 50 percent
- 45 percent No

Adults
- Yes 32 percent
- 60 percent No
- 7 percent Don't know

"Sometimes families don't want to go through a trial," Etzel said.

Society, in general, turns a blind eye toward this behavior and does not consider the men involved sexual predators when involved with teenage girls. The societal perception often changes when older man prey upon younger boys.

Some experts say prosecution of the men in teenage pregnancy cases would serve as a prevention tool.

"We've got to get a message out to everyone that this does occur, that this does happen in our society and hold perpetrators accountable," said Patrick.

But not everyone agrees.

Cara Smith, deputy chief of staff at the Illinois Attorney General's office, said there is not enough evidence to suggest that. "I don't think you can make the correlation."

TEN

Adult Men Should Be Prosecuted for Impregnating Underage Girls

Tim Potter

In the following selection *Wichita (KS) Eagle* reporter Tim Potter draws readers' attention to criminal issues surrounding teen pregnancy. Using Sedgwick County, Kansas, as a study in microcosm, Potter points out that pregnancy among girls under the state's age of consent is evidence of crimes that need investigating. Speaking with law enforcement officials and others in the legal system, Potter shows how police and prosecutors are not interested in putting other teenagers on trial per se, but rather are looking to go after adult sexual predators, abusers, and gang members who rape young women— whether these be adults or teenagers. Attention is given to the murder of an underaged pregnant teen allegedly contracted by the father of the unborn child.

From 2000 through 2004, 985 Kansas girls ages 11 to 15 gave birth.

More than a quarter of them—247—were Sedgwick County residents, according to birth certificate records compiled by the Kansas Department of Health and Environment [KDHE].

Tim Potter, "Underage Pregnancy Evidence of Crime," *Wichita (KS) Eagle*, July 16, 2006.

And every one of the pregnancies was evidence of a crime, prosecutors say, because a girl under 16 legally can't have sex, even if it is voluntary.

"The bottom line is it's against the law," said Kim Parker, Sedgwick County's chief deputy district attorney.

The recent [June 2006] killing of a pregnant 14-year-old Wichita girl, Chelsea Brooks, has raised questions about the prevalence of underage pregnancies and how families and the system respond.

Not All Cases Are Equal

Not all instances of underage pregnancy can be prosecuted.

The severity of the crime depends in large part on the ages of the two people involved. Prosecutors are more likely to file charges in cases where the male and female are of significantly different ages or where there is evidence of coercion or force or related criminal activity.

"Most of these cases involve children who are of the same age who have made a mistake," said Kansas Attorney General Phill Kline. So many of them aren't—and shouldn't—be prosecuted, he said.

But if a 15-year-old girl becomes pregnant by a 35-year-old man, Kline said, "I'm prosecuting—that's too much of an age difference."

There was one such instance—a birth certificate saying a mother was 15 and the father was 35—in the records provided by the state. Because of privacy concerns, the agency said it couldn't release a breakdown of where each birth occurred.

Birth certificates often don't provide information on the father. In 467 of the 985 births reported, the birth certificate contained no information about the father.

That fact raises a red flag for Parker, the Sedgwick County prosecutor. It makes her wonder whether in some of those cases, the father of the baby could be guilty of incest or other crimes against children, and whether someone is intentionally leaving that information off the certificates to protect the father's identity.

The History of Statutory Rape Laws

As Michelle Oberman discusses in *Regulating Consensual Sex with Minors: Defining a Role for Statutory Rape*, the theoretical underpinnings of statutory rape laws have changed dramatically since their inception. The modern rationale for these laws is grounded in the desire to protect minors from sexual exploitation. However, when these laws originated in [the] 13th century, the primary intent was to protect the chastity of young women.

Oberman notes that the emergence of feminism heavily influenced changes to statutory rape laws. The laws went largely unchanged until the end of the 19th century, when feminists sought to increase the age of consent to protect young women from potentially coercive relationships. As a result of these efforts, the average age of consent was raised from 12 to 18 years old.

In the 1970s, second wave feminists began to challenge the underlying principles of statutory rape laws. Although they recognized the importance of protecting vulnerable minors from coercive and exploitative sexual relationships, they wanted to ensure that the laws did not unduly restrict the sexual autonomy of young women. In addition, there was a strong push to make the laws gender-neutral.

Statutory rape laws continue to evolve in the wake of the reforms of the past 30 years. For example, the issue surfaced during debates about welfare reform in the mid-1990s when some legislators suggested that stricter enforcement of statutory rape laws could help to reduce teen pregnancy rates.

Taken from: Asaph Glosser, Karen Gardiner, and Mike Fishman, *Statutory Rape: A Guide to State Laws and Reporting Requirements.* Prepared for the Office of the Assistant Secretary for Planning and Evaluation, Department of Health and Human Services, December 15, 2004. www.4parents.gov/sexrisky/statutoryrapelaws.pdf.

In most cases, Parker said, the girls giving birth know who the father is.

Sometimes, prosecutors say, pregnant girls or their families feel pressure not to provide birth certificate information.

And in some cases, Kline said, the ages of the fathers could be wrongly reported on purpose.

Cases Are Based on the Girls' Ages

Of the reported fathers on the statewide birth certificates, the biggest concentration—356—were ages 16 to 19.

The youngest fathers were 14; the oldest was 35.

The youngest mother was 11. The numbers markedly rose as the girls got older: three 12-year-old mothers, 38 13-year-olds, 193 14-year-olds and 750 15-year-olds.

Prosecutors base their cases on a girl's age at the time of the intercourse or sexual activity.

Of the reported fathers in Sedgwick County, 38 were 19 and older, the records show. Parker said she couldn't say how many of those men were prosecuted because case files aren't sorted by pregnancies and the age of the father.

But each year, she said, the Sedgwick County district attorney's office prosecutes 65 to 70 cases of sex crimes against children, including rape, indecent liberties and solicitation.

Birth certificates aren't the only measure of underage pregnancy. According to KDHE records, 466 Kansas girls under 16 received abortions in the state during the same five-year period. There were two still-births to girls under 16 during that period. Miscarriages are not tracked.

Weighing Other Factors

Many variables determine whether prosecutors will file charges based on an underage pregnancy.

Even if the two people involved are both 15, for example, the father could still be charged if he has a pattern of criminal activity or has impregnated other girls, Parker said. Some gang initiations —called "jumping in"—involve having sex. That's the kind of thing that could get a young father prosecuted, Parker said.

The ability to bring charges can hinge on whether law enforcement agencies learn of a pregnancy. Underage pregnancies are supposed to be reported by a list of people including teachers, school administrators, therapists, doctors, nurses and social workers. Their role is important because families sometimes choose not to report those pregnancies.

But sometimes the so-called "mandatory reporters" don't follow through. Parker said she's concerned that some teachers don't report sexual activity, including pregnancy, because they don't want to see young people face prosecution. Sometimes, she said, teachers might report a pregnancy to an administrator, but the administrator doesn't follow through. The system doesn't make it easy for teachers to report, she said.

Intervention is important, police and prosecutors say, because too often families try to keep an underage pregnancy quiet. They might be embarrassed. They might want to spare their daughter from being a key witness. They might want to protect the father.

Sometimes the girl's family has supported or tolerated the relationship.

A Family Problem

Part of the problem is that in many cases, families don't think of a daughter's pregnancy as a crime. In their minds, says Wichita police [captain] Randy Landen, "It's a family problem, a social situation. It's not a crime."

And it's difficult for police to investigate when the girls aren't willing witnesses.

DNA, taken from a baby after birth, can be used to show paternity and can help prosecutors make a case.

In the case of Chelsea Brooks, the 14-year-old who was strangled and whose body was left in a shallow grave, there were allegations before her death that she was a victim of underage sex. Authorities were waiting for her to give birth so they could conduct a paternity test, District Attorney Nola Foulston has said.

The charges allege that Chelsea, who was nine months pregnant, was the victim of a contract killing involving her baby's alleged father. Prosecutors have charged 20-year-old Elgin "Ray-Ray" Robinson Jr., the man who reportedly was the baby's father, and two other men with capital murder.

[In July 2006], 17-year-old Everett Gentry pleaded guilty to capital murder in the death.

Under a plea agreement, Gentry will testify, if needed, against Robinson and Theodore G. Burnett, 49.

At [the] hearing, Gentry told District Judge Greg Waller that Robinson had requested the killing. Gentry said Burnett did the job for $500.

In addition to capital murder, Robinson also is charged with two counts of rape; he is accused of having sex with Chelsea before she turned 14.

In her case, her family intervened months before her death. Her mother obtained a protective order against Robinson and filed court documents accusing him of impregnating her daughter.

The murder of Kansas teen fourteen-year-old Chelsea Brooks by her older boyfriend highlights the need for prosecutors to go after adult sexual predators and abusers of teenage girls.

A Successfully Prosecuted Case

In a recent Butler County case, DNA evidence proved crucial when a 19-year-old man pleaded guilty after a DNA swab identified him as the father of a 15-year-old's child. The man was 18 when he impregnated the mentally disabled girl, said Darrin Devinney, an assistant Butler County attorney.

The girl's mother became suspicious when her daughter said she no longer needed feminine hygiene products. She found out her daughter was pregnant, Devinney said, and the family reported it to authorities.

The man pleaded guilty to unlawful voluntary sexual relations. Depending on his criminal history, he could face probation or up to nearly two years in prison.

There was no indication he was taking advantage of the girl because of her disability, Devinney said. Otherwise, he would have been charged with rape.

The records showed that Butler County had 13 underage pregnancies in the five-year period. Devinney, who handles cases involving crimes against children, estimated that prosecutors were able to file charges in half of those 13 instances.

In Harvey County over the same five years, there were six births to girls 15 and younger, the records show.

ELEVEN

Contraceptive-Based Sex Education Reduces Teen Pregnancy

Amy Schalet

In the following selection assistant professor of sociology at the University of Massachusetts–Amherst Amy Schalet points out the failures of abstinence-only sex education curricula in preventing teen pregnancy. Such approaches to sex education discourage honest conversation, which she states is necessary in adequately addressing the issues surrounding teen sexuality. Young people today, she contends, are living in a social/sexual environment very different from that of earlier generations, which makes it more difficult for them to deal with unintended pregnancies. Schalet proposes a different approach: one like that of the Netherlands, which, although teens there become sexually active at about the same time as teens in the United States, has one of the lowest rates of teen pregnancy among the developed nations. The Netherlands provides teens with access to information and contraceptives.

Sarah Palin faced a variety of questions at last week's debate [October 2, 2008], but not the one I would have asked:

"Should public school students be taught that contraception and condoms can prevent unintended pregnancy and disease?"

Palin has referred to her teenage daughter's pregnancy as a normal "up and down" of family life. Sympathetic politicians and commentators, including Bill Clinton, have concurred, attributing teenage pregnancies to "raging hormones" and saying that since the couple plans to marry, Bristol Palin's pregnancy is really an early awakening to adult responsibilities.

Abstinence-Only Sex Education Discourages Conversation

But left obscured by the raging-hormones explanation is the fact that teen pregnancy is far from inevitable. Like some other controversies at the heart of the culture wars, this problem—which, after receding nationally since the early 1990s, appears to be worsening again—need not exist. High teen pregnancy rates result in part from our inability to talk honestly and wisely about teen sexuality. And they are exacerbated by policies that prohibit such talk.

American teenagers grow up in environments that inhibit them from making conscious choices about sex and using contraception effectively. Sarah Palin supports programs that contribute to that environment, favoring policies that prohibit teachers from explaining the benefits of contraception and condoms and that require teaching that sex outside of marriage is unacceptable.

Such "abstinence-until-marriage" policies are built on the myth of a past when people did not have sex until they were married and, this thinking goes, prevented many of the troubles that plague society today. But for more than half a century, the majority of Americans have been having premarital sex. In the 1950s, one in three teenage mothers conceived out of wedlock. And many "shotgun" marriages ended in divorce.

Teenage parents face an even taller order today; it is no longer as easy for a man without a college degree to get a well-paying job to provide for a family, and young women rightly expect to pursue their talents both inside and outside the home, a challenge to pull off without higher education.

Many experts say that teenagers benefit from an environment that encourages adults to explain the benefits of contraception and condoms.

Simply put, the circumstances and aspirations of young people have changed since the 1950s, but our society's narratives about the place of sexuality and the nature of relationships do not reflect these changes. And we pay a price for that inability to talk realistically about teenage sexuality and love.

Different Attitudes Bring Different Results

Just how steep, and unnecessary, that price is becomes clear when we look at countries where teenagers do not pay it. In the Netherlands, young people become sexually active at the same age as their American and other counterparts across the developed world—around 17—but teenage pregnancy rates are six times lower than they are here.

In 1950s Dutch society, most young people began having sex when they were in their 20s and were married or engaged. During the 1960s, unintended teenage pregnancies rose alarmingly. Seeing this, family physicians and clinics were quick to make contraceptives easily accessible to youth. Dutch teen pregnancy and abortion rates are now among the lowest in the developed world.

National surveys show that most Dutch parents accept that young people choose to have sex in committed relationships during their later teens. Research I conducted found that a majority of Dutch parents are even willing to permit such couples to spend the night together in their homes, but only when they see that they have formed a loving relationship, feel ready for sex and understand how to use contraception responsibly. By accepting teen sexuality within these parameters, Dutch parents can stay involved, monitor relationships and urge proper contraceptive use.

Parents Adapted to Changing Times

This shift from a "marriage-only" to a "love-only" sexual ethic happened because parents, aided by honest and informative public conversations about sex, grappled with how to marry their aspirations—about the children they wanted to raise and the relationships they wanted to foster—to times that were changing.

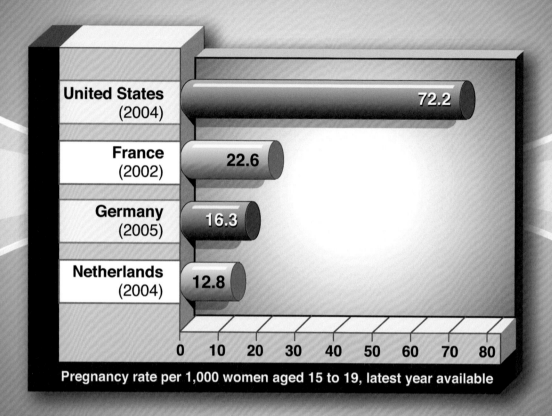

Adolescent Pregnancy Rates in the United States Exceed Those in Europe

Country	Rate
United States (2004)	72.2
France (2002)	22.6
Germany (2005)	16.3
Netherlands (2004)	12.8

Pregnancy rate per 1,000 women aged 15 to 19, latest year available

Taken from: Ammie Feijoo, Sue Alford, and Deb Houser, Advocates for Youth, "Adolescent Sexual Health in Europe and the U.S.—Why the Difference?" Third edition. www.advocatesforyouth.org/PUBLICATIONS/factsheet/fsest.pdf.

The result is an environment in which young people receive support from parents and other adults as they learn about relationships and wise sexual choices.

American teenagers lack such an environment. All too often, they feel sex is a secret that can ruin their lives. Bristol Palin's pregnancy does little to dispel the fear that the risks of sex cannot be controlled. With impending parenthood a surely unintended byproduct of her youthful experiences, at age 17 hers is a life constrained in ways that few of us would want for ourselves or our loved ones.

The Palins, of course, deserve credit for their public embrace of their eldest daughter, which shows that, ideology notwithstanding, parents still love their daughters even if they have sex. If that embrace allays fears that prompt girls to keep sex a secret from their parents, then the Republican Party may have, inadvertently, facilitated the honest conversations we need to move beyond the myth-only approach to adolescent sexuality.

TWELVE

Contraceptive-Based Sex Education Is Ineffective for Intentional Teen Pregnancies

Daniel P. Moloney

In the following viewpoint Daniel P. Moloney, senior policy analyst at the Heritage Foundation's Richard and Helen DeVos Center for Religion and Civil Society, shows contraceptive-based sex education curricula to be ineffective, especially since such curricula do not address the issue of intentional pregnancies among teen girls. Girls may choose to become pregnant in an effort to meet deeper emotional needs in their own lives. Moloney argues that to offer more contraceptives to girls wanting to become pregnant is both ineffective and a waste of financial resources.

Most experts concerned about teen pregnancy assume that teenage girls don't want to get pregnant. So, they assume, the logical way to reduce teen pregnancy is to teach the girls how to avoid getting pregnant, whether through abstinence or

Daniel P. Moloney, "Planned Teen Parenthood," The Heritage Foundation, July 2, 2008. Reproduced by permission.

contraception. Almost all campaigns to reduce teen pregnancy are based on this premise. Unfortunately, that assumption and the policies based on it are often wrong, as recent news reminds us. A high school in Gloucester, Massachusetts, a harbor town 30 miles outside Boston, saw a sudden spike in the number of pregnant students—18 by the end of this school year [2007–2008], more than four times the previous year's total. *Time* [magazine] initially reported that the spike was due to a group of female students, most under the age of 16, who made a "pact" to get pregnant:

It can be argued that incidents such as the Gloucester High School pregnancy pact prove that teaching contraception to teenage girls who want to become pregnant does not work.

School officials started looking into the matter as early as October [2007] after an unusual number of girls began filing into the school clinic to find out if they were pregnant. By May [2008], several students had returned multiple times to get pregnancy tests, and on hearing the results, "some girls seemed more upset when they weren't pregnant than when they were," [Principal Joseph] Sullivan says. All it took was a few simple questions before nearly half the expecting students, none older than 16, confessed to making a pact to get pregnant and raise their babies together.

Officials had reason to be frustrated. Gloucester High had a school-based health clinic; they had contracted with the local Title X family planning clinic to provide comprehensive sex-ed classes, they even offered an elaborate program of free day care in a converted classroom to help mothers stay in school. They did everything by the book, and the spike in pregnancies occurred anyway. Why?

Former classmate Amanda Ireland may have the answer. According to *Time*: "Ireland, 18, gave birth her freshman year and says some of her now pregnant schoolmates regularly approached her in the hall, remarking how lucky she was to have a baby. 'They're so excited to finally have someone to love them unconditionally,' Ireland says."

Pregnancy Brings Meaning

This explanation dovetails with the research of sociologists Kathryn Edin and Maria Kefalas in their book *Promises I Can Keep: Why Poor Women Put Motherhood Before Marriage*. Edin and Kefalas spent five years living in the same neighborhoods with poor unwed mothers. Their conclusions are often counterintuitive. For example:

While the poor women we interviewed saw marriage as a luxury, something they aspired to but feared they might never achieve, they judged children to be a necessity, an absolutely essential part of a young woman's life, the chief source of identity and meaning.

Local news reports have questioned *Time*'s characterization of the situation, but nobody is denying that these girls knew how to avoid getting pregnant and instead chose otherwise. To young girls who see teenage pregnancy as something desirable, making a pact like this is not unimaginable.

Local health officials in Gloucester, however, seem to have been completely oblivious to the aspirations of these girls. Gloucester High offers pregnancy tests and other reproductive health services through its school-based health clinic. At least some of the girls clearly were happy to be pregnant—slapping high fives when they heard the news—which suggests they weren't trying to avoid conception. Yet the nurse who runs the clinic and the clinic's medical director reacted by calling for greater access to birth control, even if the parents of the girls didn't approve:

> [B]y May, after nurse practitioner Kim Daly had administered some 150 pregnancy tests at Gloucester High's student clinic, she and the clinic's medical director, Dr. Brian Orr, a local pediatrician, began to advocate prescribing contraceptives regardless of parental consent, a practice at about 15 public high schools in Massachusetts.

Parents might be wondering how it could be legal for schools to offer contraceptives to minors without their parents' consent. And how could this be the practice at over one-quarter of the school-based health clinics in Massachusetts? Because federal and state laws usually require that publicly funded health clinics offer birth control and other reproductive health services to minors who request them, without parental consent or notice. . . .

Birth Control Is Not the Answer

Prescribing contraceptives without parental notification or consent is common practice at school health clinics. In fact, federal law requires

The Main Reasons Teens Do Not Use Contraceptives

What do you think is the main reason teens do not use birth control or protection when they have sex?

Reason	Percentage of Teens (aged 12–19)
Are afraid their parents might find out	18
Simply decide not to	14
Some other reason	12
Don't know any better	10
Are under the influence of drugs or alcohol	10
Have difficulty getting birth control or prevention	9
Feel pressure not to	5
Don't know	4
Cannot afford birth control or protection	3
Have religious or personal beliefs that oppose birth control or protection	1

Taken from: Bill Albert, *With One Voice 2007: America's Adults and Teens Sound Off About Teen Pregnancy; A Periodic National Survey*, February 2007. Copyright 2007 by the National Campaign to Prevent Teen Pregnancy. www.thenationalcampaign.org/resources/pdf/pubs/WOV2007_fulltext.pdf.

it when the minor is eligible for Medicaid, or when the clinic receives Title X funds. The policy is based on the belief that requiring parental consent before a girl can get birth control won't reduce teen sexual activity at all. Because the parents may say no and because teens will, presumably, "do it anyway," requiring consent only makes it more likely that the girl would get pregnant or contract a disease.

This view is unproven, but it has been the foundation of U.S. family planning policy since 1972. And the push to expand school-based health clinics is part of a movement to increase the availability of birth control to minors without their parents' knowledge or consent.

It's difficult to imagine a more counterproductive approach. These girls need more parental involvement, not less. These young girls *know how* to have babies, so further sex ed isn't needed. They *want* to have babies, so contraception is beside the point. The problem is that they think that they *are ready* to have babies, and they aren't.

That's where the parents should be stepping in, helping the girls to realize that they aren't ready to be mothers. Social-science data clearly shows that teenage motherhood is frequently a ticket to a life of poverty.

Parents Need Information

Studies show that teens are less likely to have sex if they think their parents disapprove. But parents are often kept in the dark, thanks to misbegotten health care policies which view them as a threat to their daughter's best interests.

Our nation's "experts" are spectacularly ill-equipped to deal with teenage girls who want to be mothers. Indeed, laws designed to make contraceptives available to teenagers often make the problem worse. Lawmakers should change these policies—and give parents the opportunity to teach their children well.

THIRTEEN

Abstinence-Based Sex Education Is Ineffective and Harmful to Teens

Jeff Stryker

Jeff Stryker works for the Center for AIDS Prevention Studies at the University of California–San Francisco. In the following article, Stryker finds that, despite the rise in abstinence-only sex education funding at all levels of government, there is no evidence that this approach works. Stryker notes that the abstinence-only argument is based on the flawed idea that sex education actually encourages sexual activity. To combat the high numbers of teenagers who are pregnant or have a sexually transmitted disease, researchers and scientists say that sex education programs must teach safe sex behaviors, including using condoms, and discuss the biology of sex.

Just say no, or say nothing at all. That's what Shari Lo, 15, found out this past March [1997]. The Southern California high school sophomore conducted an experiment for her school's science fair, subjecting six brands of condom to laboratory tests of strength and durability. She won a first-place ribbon and an invitation to compete in a regional competition—that is, until officials at Coachella Valley Unified School District got wind of Lo's project and yanked it from the regional competition. School Superintendent Colleen Gaynes explained the misgivings about the science-fair entry: "Because it is on condom reliability, it basically encourages safe sex. Our philosophy is abstinence, not safe sex."

The Abstinence Movement

The sentiment expressed by Superintendent Gaynes is being echoed across the country, as school board after school board adopts abstinence-only sex education programs. Abstinence-only education stresses "character" and "values" ignoring contraception and safer-sex techniques, or discussing them only to underscore failure rates. Such programs are driving out more comprehensive curricular approaches and, as in Lo's case, stifling even reasoned discussions of teen sexuality.

The high-water mark of the abstinence movement is the federal welfare repeal provision for abstinence education. The legislation earmarks $50 million a year for five years for school programs that have as their "exclusive purpose" teaching the "social, psychological, and health gains" to be realized from abstinence. The block grant requires 75 percent matching funds from public or private sources, for an annual total of more than $87 million. Another federal endeavor, the Adolescent Family Life Demonstration Projects Program, has also been directed to spend about $8 million of its $14.2 million budget on abstinence-only programs. As the July 15 [1997] deadline for grant applications approaches, some states are reluctant even to apply for funds because of the strings attached.

The victory for abstinence-only organizing at the federal level caps successes at the state and local level. Increasingly, states are requiring schools to teach about abstinence, while restricting discussions of contraception, safer sex and homosexuality. At least twenty-three states now require abstinence instruction, and only eleven of these also require teaching about

Teens and adults hold a rally in favor of abstinence. However, some scientific data show that relying solely on abstinence as a birth control method is ineffective.

contraception or disease prevention. Newer restrictive laws include North Carolina's, which requires "abstinence until marriage education." Texas now compels teaching of the "emotional trauma" associated with teen sex, and South Dakota went so far as to repeal its previous mandate for AIDS education.

The abstinence movement is propelled by conservative religious groups like the Christian Coalition, broad-based "family values" organizations like Focus on the Family in Colorado Springs, Colorado, and newer, issue-specific groups such as the

Medical Institute for Sexual Health (MISH) in Austin, Texas, and the Chastity Education Network in Springfield, Pennsylvania. They have slick teaching materials with a veneer of psychological jargon and epidemiological statistics with which to seduce school boards. They certainly have the most memorable slogans: Who can forget "Pet Your Dog, Not Your Date?"

What abstinence-only proponents lack is evidence that their programs work. PBS commentator Bonnie Erbe sums it up succinctly: "The Clinton administration and Congress may as well take $250 million in cash, put it through a shredder and feed it to cattle, as give it to schools to teach abstinence to high school students." The scenario is reminiscent of the nation's love affair with Drug Abuse Resistance Education (DARE), the wildly popular yet spectacularly ineffective school-based drug education program. Like their DARE counterparts, supporters of abstinence-only approaches to sex education do not seem particularly troubled by the lack of evidence from the peer-reviewed scientific literature that their programs are effective.

The Realities of Teenage Sex

The abstinence-only federal edicts are the spoils of a culture war for the control of teenagers' hearts, minds, and libidos. Fought largely on emotional grounds, abstinence-only arguments have been driven by the persistent but mistaken belief that sex education itself somehow seduces teenagers into sexual activity. It follows that schools should either ignore the issue or discuss sexuality only in terms of fear and disease, leaving no alternative to abstinence. The casualties in the culture wars are the teenagers themselves, denied information about how to prevent pregnancy or avoid sexually transmitted diseases in the highly likely event that they have sexual intercourse.

In seeking to impose their values, abstinence proponents are marshaling arguments that fly in the face of both science and human experience. For example, nestled among the eight federal abstinence education criteria is the statement "Sexual activity outside of the context of marriage is likely to have harmful psychological and physical effects." Tell that to the more than 93 percent of men and 80 percent of women between ages 18 and 59 who were not virgins on their wedding nights. The disconnect between the abstinence-until-marriage aspirations and the realities of adolescent (and adult) sexual behavior is profound. According to researchers, more than 85 percent of teenagers report having a girlfriend or boyfriend and having kissed someone romantically. By age 14, more than 50 percent of all boys have touched a girl's breast and 25 percent have touched a girl's vulva.

And many kids go all the way, experiencing what epidemiologists insist on calling the "onset of intercourse," as if it were a rash. Seventy-three percent of young men and 56 percent of young women have experienced intercourse's onset by their 18th birthday. Even among teens who have not rounded the bases (in the language of an earlier era), and who may not even be looking to hit one out of the park, there is plenty of infield activity. Recent studies have suggested that many teens, aware of the risks inherent in penetrative sex, are turning to oral sex. RAND analyst and U.C.L.A. [University of California–Los Angeles] pediatrician Mark Schuster and colleagues reported in the *American Journal of Public Health* that among 2,026 urban high school students surveyed, 47 percent were virgins. Yet about 30 percent of the high school virgins had masturbated a partner, 9 percent had engaged in heterosexual fellatio including ejaculation and 10 percent had engaged in cunnilingus. The *New York Times*, not usually a hot read, reported recently that the question seventh-grade girls most often ask is not "Where do babies come from?" but "Do you spit or do you swallow?"

What Should Be Done?

So there's a whole lot of sex going on. More than a quarter of teenage girls have had intercourse by age 15. More than 1 million U.S. teenagers become pregnant and 3 million acquire sexually transmitted diseases each year. In Canada, England, France, the Netherlands and Sweden, where the age of first intercourse is roughly the same, teen pregnancy rates are less than half those of the United States. Is there any program that can make a dent in these numbers, if only by delaying the onset of intercourse?

Not a program that focuses on abstinence alone, comes the near-universal reply from the behavioral and social science community. According to a February [1997] consensus statement on H.I.V. risks by behavioral researchers convened by the National Institutes of Health, "Although sexual abstinence is a desirable objective, programs must include instruction in safe sex behavior, including condom use." Douglas Kirby, director of research at ETR Associates in Santa Cruz, California, has conducted and catalogued research on the effectiveness of sex education for more than a decade. He maintains that federal welfare abstinence provisions represent "'politics' and unwise public policy." Kirby is no prosex radical. He scoured the social science literature for evidence of the effectiveness of abstinence-only approaches. For his most recent review, published in March [1997] by the National Campaign to Prevent Teen Pregnancy, Kirby found only six published studies of abstinence-only programs. None were effective, and one was clearly ineffective.

Kirby is modest in his claims for more comprehensive approaches. The title of his most recent report signals the field's limitations: No Easy Answers: Research Findings on Programs to Reduce Teen Pregnancy. The report sensibly acknowledges that classroom instruction must be factored in the mix with raging hormones and influences from peers, parents, churches and a media barrage of pro-sex messages. Nevertheless, a number of comprehensive sex education curriculums examined in rigorous studies have achieved modest delays in sexual intercourse or increases in contraceptive use. Although identifying many factors common to a number of successful programs, the report contends that "little evidence exists regarding which of these factors or combinations of factors contribute most to the overall success of the programs."

Clearly, the better sex education programs address more than the biology of sex and risk (although kids are owed the basic facts on how their bodies work and how to protect themselves from sexually transmitted diseases). Comprehensive sex education explores the context for and meaning involved in sex. It acknowledges that sex is a social activity involving values and choices. The best sex education begins with abstinence as a starting point, both encouraging it for young people who are not ready for sex and supporting those who choose it for whatever reason.

Critics such as Barbara Dafoe Whitehead condemn modern sex education. Her *Atlantic Monthly* cover story of 1994 concluded with the observation that "once kids have been equipped with refusal skills, a bottle of body oil, and some condoms, 'reality-based' advocates send them into the world to fend for themselves." Abstinence-only advocates want to send kids into the world with strong characters and values. Yet despite arguments by groups such as MISH that they seek to teach a "core" set of ethical values "widely shared even in our highly pluralistic society," the nature of the character and values to be stressed betrays a cramped pluralism. The message is just say no, no, no—whether 12 years old or 18. Whether the activity in question is intercourse or "outercourse" (with the distinct implication that mutual masturbation is as risky as penetrative vaginal or anal sex). Of course, gay teens do not fit in the abstinence-only world. (With the Defense of Marriage Act, what could abstinence-until-marriage mean for gays and lesbians anyway?) Homosexuality is either totally ignored or deemed, together with contraception and abortion, "too hot to handle."

That is the fray that Shari Lo inadvertently stepped into when she entered the science fair. She is a bit bewildered by all the attention. After describing her laboratory stretch tests and which condom came out on top (Class Act), she said, "It was kind of illogical for teachers to focus on abstinence alone and not safe sex."

Lo had not heard of the letter writer who rallied to her defense in the *Los Angeles Times*, but she, too, now knows that merely discussing teenage sexuality can derail a career. "Abstinence is a good thing, and it works for many of your youth," Dr.

Joycelyn Elders acknowledged. "However, I am not willing to just throw away those other youths for which it does not work for one reason or another. Shari Lo's work is important, and in a real school that was interested in her whole individual development, her ideas would not be denied."

FOURTEEN

Parental Consent Should Be Required for Abortions by Minors

Yes on 4—Sarah's Law

> The following viewpoint argues that the need for parental consent for minors to obtain an abortion extends far beyond the procedure itself. Complications from an abortion can be serious, and without the knowledge of the abortion, parents are not properly equipped to be watching for such signs. Notifying parents of an abortion may also bring possible sexual abuse to light, with parents and law enforcement officials able to work together effectively in order to bring abusers to justice. The author of this viewpoint, Yes on 4—Sarah's Law, is an organization dedicated to requiring parental notification for minors to obtain abortions, in response to the death of a fifteen-year-old girl who died due to complications from a legal abortion.

Sarah was only 15 years old when she died from a legal abortion. She was injured during the procedure and developed a massive infection. Her parents weren't told about the abortion and didn't know what was wrong with her. By the time she was taken to the hospital, it was too late. Sarah's family could have saved her—had they known.

Yes on 4—Sarah's Law, "Why California Needs Proposition 4," www.yeson4.net, 2008. Reproduced by permission.

Parental abortion notification laws like California's Sarah's Law have been vigorously opposed by pro-choice advocates.

In California, a girl under age 18 can't get a tan at a tanning salon, a cavity filled, or an aspirin dispensed by the school nurse without a parent knowing. But a doctor can perform a surgical or chemical abortion on a young girl without informing any family member.

Proposition 4 will require a doctor to notify at least one adult family member before performing an abortion on an under-18-year-old girl.

Medical professionals know that a young person is safer when a parent or family member is informed of her medical situation. Someone who knows the girl and cares about her future can help her understand all her options, obtain competent care, and work through the problems that led her into the situation to begin with.

On a daily basis, older men exploit young girls and use secret abortions to cover up their crimes.

More than thirty states currently have parental/family involvement laws like Proposition 4 in effect.

States which have laws like Proposition 4 have experienced real reductions in pregnancies and sexually transmitted diseases among young girls.

The Facts of Proposition 4

The truth is:

- Proposition 4 gives girls from abusive homes the option of having the doctor notify another adult family member—such as a grandmother, aunt, or sibling—rather than a parent.
- Despite family involvement laws being in effect in the majority of states for years, even decades, there is not any statistical data nor even a single documented anecdote of a minor being harmed by such laws.
- Abortion providers rarely report statutory rape or sexual abuse of minors to child protection services. Instead, they provide a secret, tax-funded abortion, and the young girl is returned to the same abusive relationship. *Secret abortions endanger young girls.*

Proposition 4: The Abortion Waiting Period and Parental Notification Initiative

The Waiting Period and Parental Notification before Termination of Minor's Pregnancy Initiative, Constitutional Amendment, 2008, proposes to change the California constitution to prohibit abortion for an unemancipated minor until forty-eight hours after physician notifies the minor's parent or legal guardian.

- **Permits notification to certain adult relatives if doctor reports parent to law enforcement or Child Protective Services**

- **Provides notification exceptions for medical emergency or parental waiver**

- **Permits courts to waive notice based on clear and convincing evidence of minor's maturity or best interests**

- **Mandates reporting requirements, including reports from physicians regarding abortions on minors**

- **Authorizes damages against physicians for violation**

- **Requires minor's consent to abortion, with exceptions**

Taken from: California Secretary of State, *California General Election, November 4, 2008, Official Voter Information Guide*, "Prop 4, Waiting Period and Parental Notification before Termination of Minor's Pregnancy. Initiative Constitutional Amendment." www.voterguide.sos.ca.gov/title-sum/prop4-title-sum.htm.

Election Results

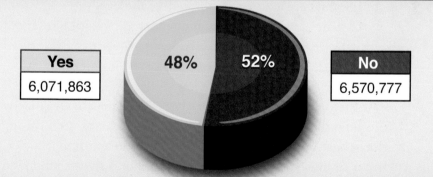

Yes	48%	52%	No
6,071,863			6,570,777

Taken from: California Secretary of State, *General Election, November 4, 2008, Election Night Results*, "Proposition 4 —Parent Notification Before Terminating Minor's Pregnancy." http://vote.sos.ca.gov/Returns/props/map19000000004.htm.

- A study of over 46,000 pregnancies of school-age girls in California found that over two-thirds were impregnated by adult men whose average age was 22.6 years.

Tragic Stories of Abuse

A Planned Parenthood affiliate in Arizona was found civilly liable for failing to report the fact that the clinic had performed an abortion on a 13-year-old girl who had been impregnated by her 23-year-old foster brother. The abortion provider did not report the crime, and the young girl was returned to the foster home where she was raped and impregnated a second time.

A father in California came home unexpectedly early from work one day to find his 15-year-old daughter had tried to commit suicide by drug overdose. Only in that way did he learn that the girl had been impregnated by her 33-year-old karate instructor.

When this predator found out his victim was pregnant, he told her he would commit suicide if she didn't have an abortion. So, against her wishes and her deeply held belief that abortion was murder, she had the abortion. Because of the grief and guilt she attempted suicide. Had her father not come home earlier than usual that day, she would have succeeded.

An Oregon abortion clinic provided an abortion to an eleven-year-old, yet failed to report the sexual abuse as required by state law. The abuse was disclosed to law enforcement only because the abortion was incomplete and the girl was subsequently taken to the hospital where a doctor reported the abuse.

A 13-year-old Ohio girl was impregnated by her high school coach, who then persuaded her to have an abortion. Planned Parenthood did not report the abuse, nor did it comply with the state's own parental notification law.

At the request of the male predator who brought her in, the clinic gave the girl a shot of Depo-Provera so he could have sex with her again right away. Three days after the abortion, the perpetrator resumed having sex with the girl, and then abandoned her. Only months later did the parents learn what had happened. The perpetrator is serving a prison sentence; Planned Parenthood disclaims all responsibility and is fighting a lawsuit by the parents.

FIFTEEN

Parental Consent Should Not Be Required for Abortions by Minors

Lauren Ralph and Claire Brindis

Throughout the United States, state legislatures and voters are considering revamping laws regarding access to abortions for minors—looking to require parents and guardians to be notified before abortions can be administered. However, an examination of the facts surrounding parental notification laws reveals that such laws are ineffective at best and dangerous to the health of teenagers at worst. The following selection presents California's ease of access to contraceptives and reproductive health clinics for minors (without requiring parental notification) as an example of how states can best keep unwanted pregnancies, abortions, and sexually transmitted diseases at a minimum. Claire Brindis is a professor in the Department of Pediatrics for the University of California–San Francisco. Lauren Ralph is a member of the research staff for the Philip R. Lee Institute for Health Policy Studies at the University of California–San Francisco.

Lauren Ralph and Claire Brindis, "Adolescents & Parental Notification for Abortion: What Can California Learn from the Experience in Other States?" Bixby Center for Global Reproductive Health, September 2008. Reproduced by permission of the author.

The U.S. pregnancy rate for 15- to 17-year-olds declined over 40% between 1990 and 2004, from 77 to 42 per 1,000 women. The birth rate declined as well: from 38 to 22 per 1,000 women aged 15 to 17 between 1990 and 2004.

These declines resulted from a combination of delayed sexual activity and increased contraceptive use among adolescents.

- Between 1988 and 2002, the percent of adolescent women ages 15 to 17 who have ever had sexual intercourse declined from 37% to 30%.

In 2005 Texas governor Rick Perry signed into law a bill that restricts late-term abortions and requires minor girls to obtain parental consent for an abortion.

- Between 1995 and 2002, the percent of adolescent women ages 15 to 17 that used contraception at most recent intercourse increased from 71% to 83%.

The abortion rate for adolescents also declined significantly. Between 1990 and 2004, the abortion rate fell over 57%: from 27 to 12 per 1,000 women ages 15 to 17.

California's adolescent pregnancy rate fell by 46% between 1992 and 2000: from 102 to 55 per 1,000 women ages 15 to 17, representing the second largest decline in the country (Hawaii's rate fell by 47%). During this same time period, the estimated abortion rate for young women ages 15 to 17 fell by 50%.

Furthermore, the teen birth rate fell by 54%, from 46 to 21 births per 1,000 women ages 15 to 17 between 1992 and 2005. California's teen birth rate now stands below the national average.

Teen Pregnancy Is Still a Problem

Despite this tremendous progress, 1 in 5 sexually active adolescents aged 15 to 17 in the US experiences an unintended pregnancy annually. In California, unintended pregnancies result in approximately 19,000 births, 16,000 abortions, and 7,000 miscarriages among 15 to 17 year olds each year.

Adolescents across all ethnic, racial, and socioeconomic groups seek abortion care. However:

- Socio-economically disadvantaged women living at or below 100% of the federal poverty level are over four times more likely than women not living below poverty to have an abortion.
- Hispanic and African American adolescents have abortions at rates that are 2 to 3.5 times higher, respectively, than non-Hispanic white adolescents, largely due to the fact that they experience higher pregnancy rates as well.
- Older youth (ages 18 to 19) have abortions at 3.5 times the rate of younger adolescents (aged 15 to 17).

Given these documented patterns, it is likely that poor adolescents and adolescents of color would bear a larger proportion of the likely impact if a parental involvement mandate was implemented.

The Experiences of Other States

Thirty-five states currently enforce parental consent or notification laws. There is tremendous variation in laws by state. . . . The recent increase in parental involvement legislation has come in concert with other forms of legislation designed to limit adolescents' access to safe and confidential reproductive healthcare. Recent studies suggest that this trend will negatively impact the health of adolescents. In one study, adolescents reported that they will discontinue using most reproductive health services if confidentiality is not guaranteed; however, they would not refrain from having sex. Additional research has demonstrated that when teens fear that confidentiality is not guaranteed, they are less likely to disclose all pertinent medical history to their medical provider and are less likely to return for necessary follow-up visits. . . .

Parental notification and consent laws delay minors' abortions. Induced abortion is one of the safest medical procedures for women in the U.S.; however, the risk of complications increases if an abortion is delayed into the 2nd trimester. Adolescent women are most likely to experience such delays, as they take an average of one week longer to identify a pregnancy and two weeks longer to seek abortion care than adult women. Parental involvement laws increase the likelihood of delay even further. For example, adolescents who obtained an abortion after Mississippi's parental consent requirements took effect were 10–20% more likely to do so in the second trimester. The odds of a 2nd trimester abortion increased significantly for young women ages 17.5 and older after implementation of Texas' parental notification law, indicating that these women delayed their abortion care well into the 2nd trimester as a consequence of parental notification requirements.

Mandated parental notification does not increase parental involvement in adolescents' abortion decisions. A comparison of adolescents visiting abortion clinics in states with (Minnesota) and without (Wisconsin) notification requirements demonstrates that adolescents involve their parents in their decision at similar rates (65% and 62%, respectively). There is no evidence that a government mandate will positively increase the frequency or quality of communication for adolescents and their families.

Reasons to Vote "No" on Parental Consent for Minors' Abortions

Parental communication on issues related to sex is strong without mandates.

- Over 70 percent of young U.S. women report discussing topics related to sex with their parents.

- In California, the vast majority (79%) of young women aged 14 to 17 reports that their parents are aware of their sexual activities.

Most young women communicate with their parents about their decision to have an abortion.

- In a study of states without parental involvement laws, a majority (61%) of young women under age 18 reported that at least one parent was aware of their decision to seek abortion care. Parental involvement was even higher among younger adolescents; over 90 percent of 14-year-olds and 74 percent of 15-year-olds reported having at least one parent involved in their decision.

A minority of young women choose not to involve their parents in their abortion decision, and they have valid concerns for doing so.

- In states without parental involvement laws, over 30 percent of young women who chose not to involve their parents cited fear of physical harm, being kicked out of the house, or other abuse as part of their reason not to tell their parents. Many others report that they choose not to involve their parents because of a difficult family situation, including drug dependency, loss of jobs, health problems, or marital strains.

Taken from: Bixby Center for Global Reproductive Health, "Adolescents & Parental Notification for Abortion: What Can California Learn from the Experience in Other States?" www.bixbycenter.ucsf.edu.

Some Will Take Steps to Avoid Communication

Rather than encourage family communication, parental notification and consent laws could increase utilization of a judicial bypass option for adolescents who cannot involve their parents. Young women can bypass parental involvement requirements by going before a judge. If the judge determines that parental involvement is not in the best interest of the minor or that the minor is mature enough to make the decision on her own, the parental involvement requirement can be waived. In 2003, 540 adolescents in Massachusetts obtained a judicial bypass in order to obtain abortion care, representing nearly 10% of all adolescents having abortions in the state that year.

The court system may be unprepared to handle judicial bypass requests from adolescents, placing the adolescent at increased risk of a delayed and potentially riskier abortion. A study of Pennsylvania's juvenile court system demonstrated that only 8 of 60 judicial court districts provided complete information to young women inquiring about the judicial bypass option. Additionally, a young woman's access to accurate information about the bypass option was largely subject to the knowledge and willingness of individuals in her local court to disclose the information.

The passage of parental notification and consent laws has been shown to increase the frequency with which adolescents travel out-of-state for abortion care. Incomplete data on travel and out-of-state abortion rates make it difficult to quantify the complete impact of travel on abortion rates; nonetheless, it is estimated that:

- In the 20 months following implementation of Massachusetts' parental consent law, half as many minors obtained an abortion as had done so prior to the law's implementation. During this same time period, more than 1800 minors (88% of the decrease in abortions) traveled to 5 neighboring states to have an abortion.
- In Mississippi, the abortion rate among minors did not significantly decline (<3%) after the state's parental consent law was implemented. Abortions occurring both in-state and out-of-state were included in the rate.

- After Missouri implemented its parental notification law, the in-state abortion rate for women under age 18 fell by 20%. During the same time period, the likelihood that a woman in this age group traveled out of state to obtain abortion care increased by 52%.

Education, Not Parental Accountability, Will Change Teen Behavior

Parental involvement laws have not been shown to change the age dynamics of relationships. Three-quarters of young women in the US choose sexual partners who are within three years of their own age. There is no evidence to support the claim that parental involvement laws will change the age dynamics of relationships or identify increased cases of sexual abuse. For example, after implementation of parental involvement laws in Texas and Arizona, the proportion of births to teen mothers involving significantly older fathers did not change. In 1999, 7.6% of fathers in birth to mothers aged 17 and under in Texas were significantly older (>=25 years). By 2003, three years after implementation of the state's parental notification requirements, that number had not changed significantly (7.2%).

Over the past decade, California has been at the forefront of successful efforts to reduce teen pregnancy and abortion rates. The state supports comprehensive family life education including key messages about both abstinence and contraception, and ensures the provision of contraceptive services for teens in a confidential manner. Adolescents in California are reporting delayed sexual activity and increases in contraceptive use. As a result, fewer adolescents experience unintended pregnancy and abortion each year. As evidenced by research from other states, requiring parental notification will likely not prevent abortion or the need for abortion, nor will it improve minors' communication with parents about abortion decisions. This research also suggests that parental notification can have the negative consequence of putting adolescents' health at risk by delaying and otherwise complicating access to care.

SIXTEEN

Adoption Is a Good Option for Teen Mothers

Becky Orr

In the following selection Becky Orr, education reporter for the *Wyoming Tribune-Eagle*, presents the story of a pregnant teen who decides her child's life will be better if she is adopted. The teen found that information on the adoption option was not easy to come by for teens. Getting the word out to teens about adoption and presenting it as providing opportunities for the unborn child, as well as the teen mother, are essential. Furthermore, teens who choose adoption for their children will need the support of family and friends.

It's not easy for Rockie Hiser to tell her story.

Her voice is strong and sincere. But there are moments when she fights back tears as she talks to the soon-to-be teen moms.

Still, she continues because she believes so strongly in her message.

She wants the teens to consider adoption and to become informed about the choice. Adoption is the decision she made for herself and her infant daughter.

"[It's] the hardest choice you'll ever make," she said, but added it was the right choice for both. "I know I made the right choice."

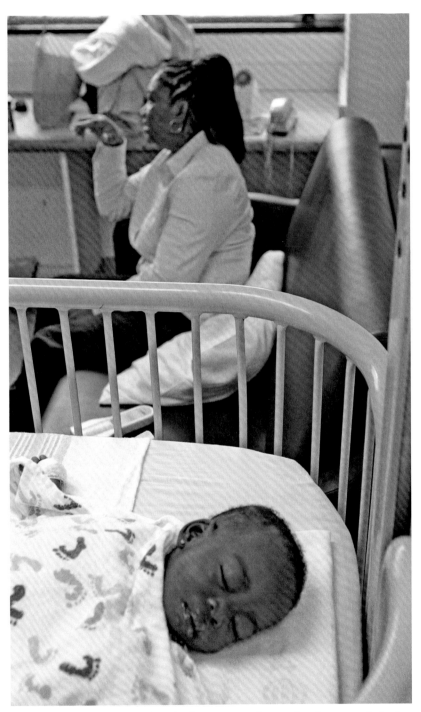

Teen mothers face difficult decisions about the future of their babies, but adoption is a good option to consider.

Deciding on adoption is not easy. She said she thinks of her daughter many times a day.

She wrote her baby a letter and made a scrapbook with pictures of herself. Both went with the infant to her new home. She hopes to see her daughter when the child turns 18.

A Lack of Information

Rockie, who is 18 now, said pregnant teens don't know much about adoption because there is a lack of information.

She checked offices of school nurses and counselors at local high schools and didn't find information. The choice was not mentioned in her high-school health class, she said. And information wasn't available at a public health clinic.

So Rockie, who graduated this year [2008] from Cheyenne's Central High, decided to send the message herself. She has launched a sophisticated campaign for young people, which includes [a] Web site, *RLifeNow.com*.

She established a scholarship foundation and a nonprofit organization called Adopt an Education, Adopt a Future. She designed colorful brochures about the program and distributed them to schools and health clinics.

Rockie wrote and published a booklet to explain her program. The publication is filled with her painstaking research about teen pregnancy. She also includes results of a voluntary and anonymous survey she conducted among 541 teens to find out their attitudes toward pregnancy and adoption.

She has a dream to raise $1 million for college scholarships for birth mothers who choose adoption. Every child deserves an education, she said, both the birth mother and the infant.

Education and future economic opportunities often are compromised when teens decide to parent, she said. Nationally, when teen mothers choose to parent, about 70 percent drop out of high school, she said.

That's compared to about 75 percent of teens who finished high school but who waited until they are 20 or 21 to have a child, based on information from the National Campaign to Prevent Teen Pregnancy.

Spreading the Word

Rockie talks to pregnant teens and other students about adoption. She has spoken at every junior high in Fort Collins [Colorado], at Colorado State University, at junior highs and high schools in Cheyenne and to adults in civic and church groups.

The term should not be "giving up a baby for adoption," she said. "It's planning for a life."

Relinquishing Children for Adoption Is Increasingly Rare

Among American children born to never-married women under 45 years old, the graph represents the percentage who were relinquished for adoption, by race, according to the year of the child's birth.

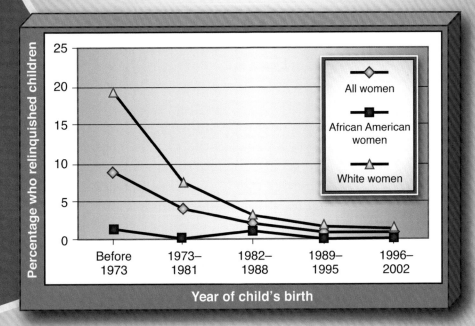

Taken from: J. Jones, "Adoption Experiences of Women and Men and Demand for Children to Adopt by Women 18–45 Years of Age in the United States," 2002. National Center for Health Statistics. *Vital Health Statistics*, series 23, no. 27, 2008. www.cdc.gov/nchs/data/series/sr_23/sr23_027.pdf.

On a recent spring afternoon, Rockie talked with pregnant teens in a [Graduation] Reality and Dual Role Skills class at Cheyenne's East High. She knows what the young women are going through.

Rockie can't talk much about the details of how she became pregnant. But one night, there was a knock at the door of the family's home in a small town.

"Two familiar faces and sexual assault entered my home," she said. She was only 15 and had the baby at 16.

She never considered abortion. Adoption offered a brighter world for herself and her baby, she said.

There's a stigma among teens that adoption is [a] selfish thing for a parent to do, she said. "But it's the exact opposite."

Instead, it's a realization that adoption means more opportunities for the child, including education, she said. She wants pregnant teen girls to understand the benefits of adoption.

But she doesn't criticize those who choose to parent. Not every option is for every girl, she said.

There are nearly half a million couples in America who want to adopt infants, she said. More than 1 million teens become pregnant each year.

Family Support Is Crucial

Her family has helped her a lot with the project, she said. Her mother, Brandi, worked with her. "She's been an awesome help," Rockie said. "I couldn't do it without them."

Brandi said she was quite astounded when her daughter suggested starting the organization. The entire family—including father Tom and younger brother Clay—are behind her.

"No matter what the situation, my family has always helped me fight my battles, tackle my dreams and soar into whatever my future may hold," Rockie said.

Rockie started her Adopt an Education program as a DECA [an association of high school and college students studying marketing] project at Central. She excelled in the marketing group.

But it became much more than that for her. "I got to thinking that I could make it a realistic organization that could really help people," she said.

She won a full scholarship to Sheridan College at the Wyoming Culinary Institute. She is working at the culinary institute now and plans to go into marketing and advertising food. She wants to own her own restaurant someday.

Central teacher Vickie Bonham teaches pregnant teens. She commends Hiser for her efforts.

"I think it's amazing. That is a tough decision for a teen to make. She has turned it into a very positive thing in her life."

Rockie said she will continue her program to encourage adoption and explaining its benefits, adding "I hope it can be part of my life forever."

SEVENTEEN

Teen Mothers Have the Right to Decide How to Handle Their Own Pregnancies

Sondra Forsyth

In the following selection journalist Sondra Forsyth presents the stories of three teens who find themselves pregnant. Even though these girls had preconceived ideas of how they might react to discovering themselves to be pregnant, it was not until they were faced with the cold truth that each of them came to realize the true complexity of the issues surrounding their pregnancies and their personal choices regarding their pregnancies. Of primary importance for any young woman in the same situation to remember is that the decisions regarding her pregnancy are hers—the law does not allow anyone else to decide whether or not to terminate the pregnancy, nor to decide whether the child should be kept by the mother or adopted.

You may think you know exactly what you'd do if you got pregnant tomorrow. Maybe you believe that abortion is immoral—something you would never even *consider*. Or maybe you've already decided that you *would* have an abortion if you

Sondra Forsyth, "Moment of Truth: Every Year, One Million American Teens Find Out They're Pregnant. What They Do Next Is the Biggest Decision of Their Lives," *CosmoGirl!* vol. 8, February 2006, p. 138-41. Reproduced by permission.

found yourself pregnant. But no matter how you feel, the law dictates that the decision is yours to make.

It wasn't always that way. Until 1973, abortion was illegal in most states unless it was medically necessary to save a woman's life. Desperate women would get illegal "back-alley" abortions, in which the surgery was performed in unsanitary conditions, often by unqualified practitioners. Many women ended up unable to have children, and some even died. Then, on January 22, 1973, in a case known as *Roe v. Wade*, the U.S. Supreme Court decided that banning abortion violated amendments to the Constitution that grant Americans a right to privacy. The Court ruled that within the first three months of pregnancy, all women have the right to choose to have an abortion. Many were furious at the decision, arguing that abortion is murder—and the "pro-choice, pro-life" debate has been heated ever since. So far, the Supreme Court has allowed abortion to remain legal—but laws are always subject to change. Last year [2005] two Supreme Court justice seats opened up, giving President George W. Bush the chance to appoint two new judges. Many expect that the new Court will review the *Roe v. Wade* ruling and consider overturning it.

So where do *you* stand on the issue? Before you answer, let go of the big-picture debate for a minute and think, if I were pregnant right now, what would I do? The reality is, you can't know for sure what you'd do in any situation until you're actually *there*—when you face your moment of truth. One million teens face that moment each year when they find out they're pregnant. Some are called murderers because they choose to have an abortion; others are told they're ruining their lives because they choose to keep the baby. But no matter what anyone else thinks, it's how *they* feel about their decision that's most important. Here are three girls and their moments of truth.

Cynthia Bragg, 18, from Newport News, Virginia, Got Pregnant

Cynthia had always believed that abortion should be legal—but she never thought she could ever actually have one.

I had sex for the first time about a month before my 16th birthday, in September 2002. My boyfriend and I had been dating for only a few weeks, but we'd been friends for months. I told my mom I was having sex, and she said I should go on the [birth control] Pill. Over the next year and a half, my boyfriend and I talked about what we'd do if I ever got pregnant. Even though I think women should be able to have an abortion if they want to, I was against it for myself. I'm active in my Lutheran church, and abortion just isn't something my church believes in. But it didn't matter anyway—I didn't think I'd ever actually *get* pregnant.

Then, in May 2004, I started feeling nauseous and tired all the time. When my mom said she thought I might be pregnant, I just laughed—I'd been taking the Pill every day. But my mom was worried, so she brought home three pregnancy tests. When all three were positive, I panicked. The eight months left of my pregnancy seemed like eight days, like I had no time to get my life in order so I could raise a child. I wasn't into school when I was younger—I'd dropped out of high school and gotten my GED. I eventually wanted to go to college, but in the meantime, I was working part-time in a video store—how could I raise a child?

A Difficult Choice

My boyfriend said he'd support me either way—that it was my decision. But how could I decide something like this? I was damned if I did and damned if I didn't. Then, right around that time, my friend Patricia found out she was pregnant too—and she decided to keep her baby. I started thinking about what that meant. I knew having a baby would turn my life upside down. I also knew I wasn't strong enough to give up my child for adoption and never see him or her again. In the end, I chose to have an abortion.

When I got to the clinic on June 18, 2004, about eight weeks pregnant, I started freaking out—I felt so guilty. I went through with it, though. When I woke up after the procedure, I felt empty. I don't know how else to describe it. To make matters worse, the next day my boyfriend told me he just couldn't handle everything, and he broke up with me.

For months, I was depressed and confused about what I'd done. It wasn't until Patricia had her baby in March 2005 that I started to believe I'd made the right decision. Patricia's boyfriend wasn't helping her at all financially, and she was missing out on all the fun stuff girls our age are supposed to be able to do, like going out to a late movie or taking a trip with friends. Then I look at my life—I started community college last fall, and I hope to become a nurse or a journalist someday. I'm not saying I'm proud of what I did, but I'm working toward a good future, and I probably wouldn't be where I am now if I'd had the baby. I *know* I did the right thing for me.

A number of teen mothers are capable of making informed and positive decisions affecting their pregnancies.

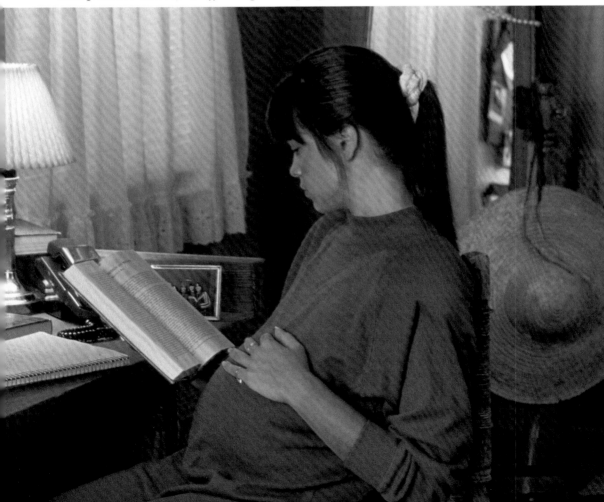

Krista Sampson, 15, from Milton, Wisconsin, Got Pregnant

When Krista and her boyfriend chose to keep the baby she was carrying, her dad checked her into a psychiatric hospital.

My boyfriend, Steven, and I had been going out for a few weeks when we started talking about having sex. We decided that when we did, we'd use a condom for birth control. But in the moment—a night in August 2004, when I was 14 and he was 17—we got carried away and didn't end up using one.

By early October, my body felt weird. It's hard to explain, but I had a feeling I might be pregnant. I went to the local Women's Choice center and got tested. When the nurse sat me down and told me my test came back positive, I froze. I knew I couldn't have an abortion—there was no way I was going to kill an innocent baby because of a mistake I had made. I figured I could give it up for adoption, but I wasn't sure I'd be able to part with my baby. I didn't know *what* to do. I figured I'd talk to Steven and find out what he thought—but I was sort of afraid he might leave me. It turned out he was really happy about the news. He didn't want to give the baby up, and he asked me to marry him. I was relieved that he was so supportive. And even though I told him I thought we were too young to get married, I decided to keep the baby.

I was terrified to tell my parents—they didn't even know I was having sex. When I did, my dad started screaming at me, saying I was making a huge mistake. My mom stayed out of it—I think she was in shock. But my dad wouldn't let it go. He actually checked me into a mental health facility by convincing the doctors that I was suicidal. I wasn't—and after a week of talking to me about my pregnancy, the doctors realized that my dad just disagreed with my decision, so they sent me home. At that point, my parents had no choice but to accept that I was keeping the baby.

Mixed Feelings

In January 2005, when I was five months pregnant and showing, some kids at school looked at me weird. But I ignored them—my *real* friends were there for me. I was excited about becoming a

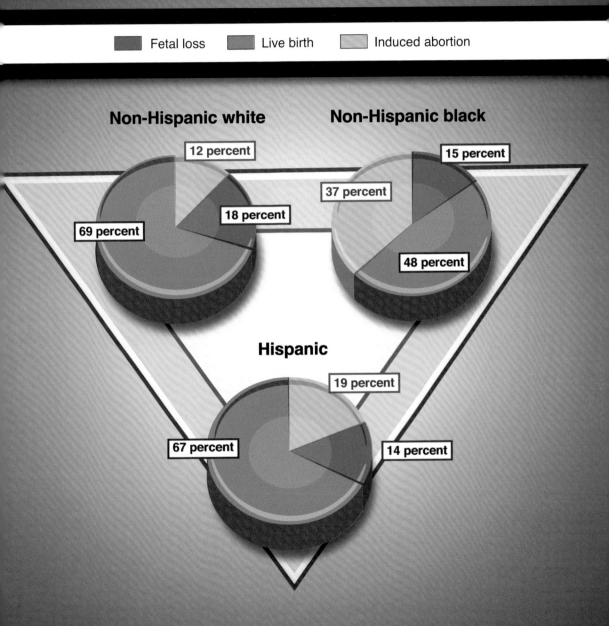

The Outcomes of Pregnancies in the United States, 2004

Fetal loss   Live birth   Induced abortion

Non-Hispanic white

12 percent

18 percent

69 percent

Non-Hispanic black

15 percent

37 percent

48 percent

Hispanic

19 percent

67 percent

14 percent

Taken from: S.J. Ventura et al., "Estimated Pregnancy Rates by Outcome for the United States, 1990–2004," *National Vital Statistics Reports;* vol. 56, no. 15. Hyattsville, MD: National Center for Health Statistics, 2008. www.cdc.gov/nchs/data/nvsr/nvsr56/nvsr56_15.pdf.

mom, in love with my boyfriend, and happy that my parents had stopped trying to convince me that I was making a mistake. But in February 2005, when I was almost six months along, I got horrible news: My mom, who had been diagnosed with breast cancer in 2003 but had gone into remission, found out that the cancer was back and she only had a few months to live.

My mom passed away on April 13, 2005—and eight weeks later, on June 7, I gave birth to a girl, Karmen Marie. It was so weird at first—I was so happy to see my daughter but so sad that my mom wouldn't get to meet her. Once my dad saw Karmen, he was completely won over. He doesn't want our family to fall apart, especially now that my mom is gone. The baby and I live with my dad, and Steven lives with his mom, who's supportive of our decision. He and I are no longer together—it's on and off like many relationships are—but he adores our baby and works at a pizza shop to help support her. He plans to go to technical school so he can get a better job someday, but now he's doing the best he can. I'm still in high school—I transferred to an alternative school that lets me bring Karmen with me. I plan to go to college. It won't be easy, but I'm determined to make it happen.

If I had it to do over, I would have waited to have sex—and I would have used birth control. I love my daughter, but I never get to hang out with my friends anymore. Still, I'm glad I stuck by my beliefs. I'd never be able to live with myself if I had an abortion. And no matter what I have to give up in order to raise Karmen, it's worth it to me.

Zoey Brooks, 19, from Sayereville, New Jersey, Got Pregnant

Zoey was 18 when she was raped at a fraternity party by a guy she'd never met. She didn't think things could get any worse—then she found out she was pregnant.

My parents were born in Zimbabwe, which is a really poor country. Growing up, I tried to live my life in a way that would make them proud. My father was always telling me how happy he was that I was in college, studying pre-law. So in April 2005, toward the end of my freshman year, my friends and I went to a fraternity party, but I decided not to drink. I'd heard that frat parties can get pretty wild, and I wanted to be on my toes. It ended up being a lot of fun—except for the fact that this one guy I wasn't interested in kept hitting on me. I felt like I was spending the whole night trying to avoid him.

At around 2 A.M., my friends went to wait in line for the bathroom before we left, so I decided to get our coats. They were piled on a table in a room downstairs, and the minute I stepped into the room I could feel somebody behind me. I turned around and saw the guy who had been hitting on me. I figured he was just coming in to get his coat, but I headed for the door because I didn't want to deal with him flirting with me again. That's when he blocked my way, grabbed me, and told me not to scream. The next thing I knew, his hand was over my mouth, I started fighting, but he was too strong. He shoved me down on a sofa behind the table, pulled my pants down, and raped me. I just cried the whole time, praying someone would come to get their coat. When he was done, he pulled up his pants and left. I lay there for a few minutes in shock, then got the coats and went to look for my friends.

I Was in Shock

On the walk home, I pretended like nothing had happened—I couldn't bring myself to believe it, let alone talk about it. When I finally confided in a friend back at my dorm, she said I should take the morning-after pill so I wouldn't get pregnant. The clinic was closed the next day, so first thing Monday morning I went and got the pill. I was told it was 97 percent effective if taken within 72 hours after sex, so I figured I'd be fine since it hadn't even been 48 hours yet. I decided not to report the rape because I didn't want my parents to know—I didn't want *anyone* to know. I just wanted to erase it from my life.

But a few weeks later, my period was five days late. That's not so unusual for me, but I took a pregnancy test to be sure. It came out positive. My very first thought was how disappointed my father was going to be. His sister had gotten pregnant when she was a teenager, and he'd warned me not to let that happen to me because it would ruin my chances for a good future. How could I tell him it *had* happened to me? I knew it wasn't my fault, but it didn't matter —I couldn't bear the thought of breaking his heart.

I had to have an abortion—it was the only way I could see not disappointing my parents. When I went home from college in May, seven weeks pregnant, I went to the clinic without telling my parents and had it done. I spent the rest of the summer keeping busy so I wouldn't think about it, but by August I was having nightmares—I'd dream that I was five months pregnant but the baby wasn't kicking. I started seeing a therapist when I got back to school, and she has helped me deal with both the abortion and the rape. Although I still have days when I feel guilty, I'm starting to forgive myself. I just hope that people try harder not to judge the choices others make. Because until something happens to you, you have no idea *how* you'll feel about it.

What You Should Know About Teen Pregnancy

The Prevalence of Teen Pregnancy

According to the Guttmacher Institute:

- The rate of teen pregnancy is significantly higher in the United States than in many other developed countries. It is two times the rate in England and Wales or Canada and eight times as high as in Japan or the Netherlands.
- Most teen pregnancies are unplanned—82 percent. Teen pregnancies account for about one in five of all unintended pregnancies in the United States.
- Every year close to 750,000 teens ages fifteen to nineteen become pregnant, and 75 of every 1,000 pregnancies occur within this age group.
- Eighteen- and nineteen-year-olds account for two-thirds of all teen pregnancies.
- In the United States the teen pregnancy rate is highest among black women (134 per 1,000 women ages fifteen to nineteen), followed by Hispanics (131 per 1,000) and non-Hispanic whites (48 per 1,000).
- Overall the teen pregnancy rate has decreased 36 percent since peaking in 1990.
- Pregnancy among black teens saw an even greater decrease (40 percent) during the same time period.
- The majority of the decline is credited to more consistent contraceptive use. Some credit is also given to more teens delaying sexual activity.

Trends in Teen Birth Rates

Information released from the National Center for Health Statistics reports:

- In 2006 the teen birth rate in the United States increased for the first time in fifteen years. In 2005 there were 41.9 births per 1,000 teens ages fifteen to nineteen, up 3 percent from 2005, when the rate was 40.5 per 1,000.
- Among eighteen- to nineteen-year-olds, this rate increased by 4 percent.
- Despite the increase the overall teen birth rate was still 32 percent lower than the peak of 61.8 in 1991 and 12 percent lower than the 2000 rate of 47.7.
- The birth rate of teens in the United States is still higher than that of any other developed country.

Negative Outcomes Associated with Teen Pregnancy

Educational and Financial:

According to StayTeen.org:

- Almost half of all teens have never thought about how a pregnancy would affect their lives.
- Parenthood is the leading reason teen girls drop out of school; less than half of the teens who become mothers ever finish high school.
- Less than 2 percent of women who become pregnant during their teen years finish college.
- Children born to teen mothers tend to have more difficulties in school than those born to older mothers: They are 50 percent more likely to repeat a grade in school, they are less likely to finish high school, and they do not perform as well on standardized tests.
- Boys born to teen mothers are twice as likely to end up in prison as are boys born to women in their twenties or older.
- Most men who father a child by a teenager will not marry the young woman; eight out of ten men do not marry the pregnant teenage mother, and the typical father in such settings pays less than eight hundred dollars per year in child support because he is living in poverty himself.

- Two out of three families begun by a teenaged mother live in poverty; more than half of all mothers on welfare began motherhood in their teens.
- Daughters born to teen mothers are three times more likely than girls born to women in their twenties or older to become teen mothers themselves.

Medical:

The March of Dimes Foundation warns of the following risks to teen mothers and their babies:

- Anemia, high blood pressure, and premature labor are more common among pregnant teens. Mothers under fifteen years old are at an even greater risk.
- Low birth weight babies and premature birth are more common among teen mothers. In 2006, 10 percent of babies born to mothers ages fifteen-to-nineteen had low birth weight, compared to babies born to mothers of all ages (6.8 percent). Even more, about 11.7 percent of babies born to fifteen-year-old mothers, had a low birth weight.
- Extremely low birth weight babies (less than 3.3 pounds, or 1.5 kg) are more than one hundred times as likely to die, and moderately low birth weight babies (3.3 to 5.5 pounds, or 1.5 to 2.5 kg) are more than five times as likely to die, before age one than normal weight babies.
- Death before age one is more likely among babies born to teen mothers than among babies born to women in their twenties and thirties.
- Death before age one is most likely among babies born to mothers under age fifteen. In 2005, 16.4 per 1,000 babies of mothers under age fifteen died versus 6.8 per 1,000 babies of mothers of all ages.

Furthermore, according to the March of Dimes Foundation, teen mothers are more likely to smoke, receive inadequate prenatal care, and to contract sexually transmitted diseases (STDs), putting their babies at risk in the following ways:

Smoking:

- Teens are more likely to smoke during pregnancy than women over age twenty-five.

- Seventeen percent of fifteen- to nineteen-year-olds smoke during their pregnancies, compared with 10 percent of twenty-five- to thirty-four-year-olds.
- Pregnancy complications, premature birth, low birth weight, and sudden infant death syndrome (SIDS) are all more likely in babies whose mothers smoked during pregnancy.

Lack of prenatal care:
- Teens are least likely to get early and regular prenatal care.
- On average, 7.1 percent of teen mothers received late or no prenatal care, compared with 3.7 percent for all ages.

STDs:
- Although they account for only one-quarter of the sexually active population, fifteen- to twenty-four-year-olds account for almost half of all new cases of sexually transmitted diseases (9.1 million—or 48 percent—of the 18.9 million new cases annually).
- Syphilis can cause blindness, infant death, and maternal death.
- Chlamydia can cause eye infections and pneumonia in newborns.
- HIV, the virus that causes AIDS, can be passed from mother to baby; however, early detection and treatment during pregnancy significantly reduces that risk.

What You Should Do About Teen Pregnancy

Be Curious

Some adults feel that only abstinence should be taught in public schools and that handing out condoms to teens will encourage them to have sex. Other adults fear that abstinence-only sex education is impractical and leaves out significant medical information. Sex education in health class at school is informative, but at the same time, most teens probably leave class with more questions than answers. Sex and sexuality is a rather large topic, after all.

If you are left with questions, do not guess. Be curious. The good news is that information is easier than ever to come by these days. Many good books about sex, written especially for teens, are available. Hopefully, your public library, school library, or local bookstore carries some. If not, the Internet can be a good place to look for answers. Of course, the Internet contains both information and misinformation, but most teens are smart enough to look at the source of the information and determine an authoritative, medically sound source from Internet junk. Three informative sites written for teens are Go Ask Alice, Columbia University's health question-and-answer Internet service; Stay Teen, a Web site for teens from the National Campaign to Prevent Teen and Unplanned Pregnancy; and It's Your Sex Life, part of Think MTV.com.

Most people, when looking for any kind of information, first ask a person they already know. Parents can be a good source of information, as can health-care providers. Older friends, relatives, and siblings that you feel safe with are usually happier to answer questions than you think. As with any source of information, however, if an answer does not seem right or if you have any doubts at all, verify it with more information.

Be Vocal

Find your voice. Talk with your friends about issues and questions. They probably have many of the same questions. On the other hand, they might have more of the answers because their parents are more open with them, or they are close to a brother or sister who has lived through similar experiences. Look up information together and share informative Internet links.

Join a youth action network. Stay Friends Action Network, for example, will e-mail you with updates on TV shows and magazines that talk about teen pregnancy, breaking news, and media contest information. If you do not want a bunch of e-mail, you can also add them as a friend to your MySpace or Facebook page.

Be an instigator—in a good sense—at your school. The National Campaign to Prevent Teen and Unplanned Pregnancy sponsors a National Day to Prevent Teen Pregnancy every year. Check it out on the campaign's Web site, talk to your teachers or school counselors, and ask them to participate. You can also participate yourself by taking part in the National Day quiz online and sending or posting the link to the quiz to your friends.

Be a political advocate. Whatever your opinion and beliefs on solutions to teen pregnancy, it is easier than ever to voice your opinion. The "Organizations to Contact" section of this book, which provides the Web sites of organizations covering the spectrum of opinions, can get you started.

Be a Friend

So, you have been curious and searched for information about sex and teen pregnancy, and you have found your voice and spoken out about teen pregnancy, but what do you do when a friend or sister delivers the news that she thinks she's pregnant? Suddenly, this is real; what to do is not so simple. What *should* you do?

Be calm. Even if she seems calm, it probably took more courage than you can imagine for her to confide in you.

Listen. Let her tell you everything she needs to. She probably needs a sympathetic ear more than she needs advice right now. She does not need judgment; she'll get enough of that from other people and probably from herself.

Be certain. If she has not been to a clinic or a doctor for a pregnancy test, encourage her to do so. Offer to go with her if she wants to make sure that she really is pregnant before she tells an adult.

Do not try to be her parent. Encourage her to confide in a parent or another safe adult—someone who cares about her and can make sure that she receives the medical care that she needs. Offer to be with her when she tells an adult, but respect her need for space if she wants to do it alone.

Try to imagine what she is going through. If you were pregnant, what would you want a friend to do or not do? Ask her if there are any specific things that you can do to help. Suggest specific ways that you could help, like walking together to stay healthy.

Respect her privacy. If she confided in you, she trusts you, and you need to respect that trust.

ORGANIZATIONS TO CONTACT

The editors have compiled the following list of organizations concerned with the issues debated in this book. The descriptions are derived from materials provided by the organizations. All have publications or information available for interested readers. The list was compiled on the date of publication of the present volume; names, addresses, phone and fax numbers, and e-mail and Internet addresses may change. Be aware that many organizations take several weeks or longer to respond to inquiries, so allow as much time as possible.

Advocates for Youth
2000 M St. NW, Ste. 750, Washington, DC 20036
(202) 419-3420
fax: (202) 419-1448
e-mail: information@advocatesforyouth.org
Web site: www.advocatesforyouth.org

Formerly the Center for Population Options, Advocates for Youth is the only national organization focusing solely on pregnancy and HIV prevention among young people. It provides information, education, and advocacy to youth-serving agencies and professionals, policy makers, and the media. Among the organization's numerous publications are the fact sheets *Adolescent Sexual Health in Europe and the U.S.—Why the Difference?* and *Adolescent Maternal Mortality: An Overlooked Crisis.* Education programs, brochures, posters, videos, reports, manuals, and policy briefs are also available on or through its Web site.

The Alan Guttmacher Institute (AGI)
125 Maiden Ln., 7th Fl., New York, NY 10038
(212) 248-1111
fax: (212) 248-1951
e-mail: www.guttmacher.org/about/info.php
Web site: www.guttmacher.org

The institute works to protect and expand the reproductive choices of all women and men. It strives to ensure people's access to the information and services they need to exercise their rights and responsibilities concerning sexual activity, reproduction, and family planning. Among the institute's publications are the periodicals *Perspectives on Sexual and Reproductive Health*, *International Family Planning Perspectives*, and *Guttmacher Policy Review*. The institute also provides media kits, fact sheets, slide presentations, reports, and statistics on its Web site as well as a "tablemaker," which will build custom statistical tables.

Child Trends, Inc. (CT)
4301 Connecticut Ave. NW, Ste. 350, Washington, DC 20008
(202) 572-6000
fax: (202) 362-8420
Web site: www.childtrends.org

CT works to provide accurate statistical and research information regarding children and their families in the United States and to educate the American public on the ways existing social trends— such as the increasing rate of teenage pregnancy—affect children. In addition to the newsletter *Facts at a Glance*, which presents the latest data on teen pregnancy rates for every state, CT also publishes fact sheets such as *Condom Use and Consistency Among Teen Males* and *What Works for Adolescent Reproductive Health: Lessons from Experimental Evaluations of Programs and Interventions*, reports, research, speeches, presentations, and briefings.

Concerned Women for America (CWA)
1015 Fifteenth St. NW, Ste. 1100, Washington, DC 20005
(202) 488-7000
fax: (202) 488-0806
Web site: www.cwfa.org

CWA's purpose is to preserve, protect, and promote traditional Judeo-Christian values through education, legislative action, and other activities. It is concerned with creating an environment that is conducive to building strong families and raising healthy children. CWA publishes the monthly *Family Voice*, which periodically addresses issues such as abortion and promoting sexual abstinence in schools.

Family Research Council
801 G St. NW, Washington, DC 20001
(202) 393-2100
fax: (202) 393-2134
Web site: www.frc.org

The council seeks to promote and protect the interests of the traditional family. It focuses on issues such as parental autonomy and responsibility, community support for single parents, and adolescent pregnancy. Among the council's numerous publications are the papers "Why Wait: The Benefits of Abstinence Before Marriage" and "Spending Too Little on Abstinence."

Focus on the Family
8605 Explorer Dr., Colorado Springs, CO 80920
(719) 531-5181
fax: (719) 531-3424
Web site: www.focusonthefamily.com

Focus on the Family is a Christian organization dedicated to preserving and strengthening the traditional family and believes that the breakdown of the traditional family is in part linked to teen pregnancy. The organization publishes *Citizen* magazine, which discusses current social issues; *Brio*, a monthly magazine for teenage girls; and online articles such as "Cause for Concern (Abstinence)" and "Sexuality Statistical Update."

Girls, Inc.
120 Wall St., New York, NY 10005
(212) 509-2000
fax: (212) 509-8708
e-mail: communications@girlsinc.org
Web site: www.girlsinc.org

Girls, Inc., is an organization for girls aged six to eighteen that works to create an environment in which girls can learn and grow to their full potential. It conducts daily programs in career and life planning, health and sexuality, and leadership and communication. Girl, Inc., publishes an e-mail newsletter, fact sheets, online articles, and action kits such as *Know Your Rights: An Action Kit for Girls.*

The Heritage Foundation
214 Massachusetts Ave. NE, Washington, DC 20002
(202) 546-4400
fax: (202) 546-8328
e-mail: info@heritage.org
Web site: www.heritage.org

The Heritage Foundation is a public policy research institute that supports the ideas of limited government and the free-market system. It promotes the view that the welfare system has contributed to the problems of illegitimacy and teenage pregnancy. Among the foundation's numerous publications is its Backgrounder series, which includes "Abstinence Education: Assessing the Evidence" and "Teen Sex: The Parent Factor," and special reports such *The Relationship Between Family Structure and Adolescent Sexual Activity.*

International TeenSTAR Program
Natural Family Planning Center of Washington, DC
TeenSTAR Program
8514 Bradmoor Dr., Bethesda, MD 20817-3810
(301) 897-9323
fax: (301) 571-5267
e-mail: hannaklaus@earthlink.net
Web site: www.teenstar-international.org

TeenSTAR (Sexuality Teaching in the context of Adult Responsibility) is geared for early, middle, and late adolescence. Classes are designed to foster understanding of the body and its fertility pattern and to explore the emotional, cognitive, social, and spiritual aspects of human sexuality. TeenSTAR publishes a bimonthly newsletter and the paper "Natural Family Planning— Is It Scientific? Is It Effective?"

National Campaign to Prevent Teen and Unplanned Pregnancy
1776 Massachusetts Ave. NW, Ste. 200, Washington, DC 20036
(202) 478-8500
fax: (212) 478-8588
Web sites: www.thenationalcampaign.org
www.TeenPregnancy.org
www.StayTeen.org

The National Campaign to Prevent Teen and Unplanned Pregnancy seeks to improve the lives and future prospects of children and families and, in particular, to help ensure that children are born into stable, two-parent families who are committed to and ready for the demanding task of raising the next generation. Its specific strategy is to prevent teen pregnancy and unplanned pregnancy among single young adults. It supports a combination of responsible values and behavior by both men and women and responsible policies in both the public and private sectors. The organization publishes national and state statistics, prepares reports such as *Another Chance: Preventing Additional Births to Teen Mothers*, and sponsors the National Day to Prevent Teen Pregnancy.

Planned Parenthood Federation of America (PPFA)
434 W. Thirty-third St., New York, NY 10001
(212) 541-7800
(212) 245-1845
Web sites: www.plannedparenthood.org
www.teenwire.com

For more than ninety years, Planned Parenthood has promoted an approach to women's health and well-being that is based on respect for each individual's right to make informed, independent decisions about sex, health, and family planning. Among PPFA's numerous publications are the research papers "The Health Benefits of Sexual Expression" and "A History of Birth Control Methods," as well as resources for educators.

Religious Coalition for Reproductive Choice
1025 Vermont Ave. NW, Ste. 1130, Washington, DC 20005

(202) 628-7700
fax: (202) 628-7716
e-mail: info@rcrc.org
Web site: www.rcrc.org

The coalition works to inform the media and the public that many mainstream religions support reproductive options, including abortion, and oppose antiabortion violence. It works to mobilize pro-choice religious people to counsel families facing unintended pregnancies. The coalition publishes articles such as "Just Say Know! Unmasking the Hidden Agenda Behind Abstinence Education" and "The Role of Religious Congregations in Fostering Adolescent Sexual Health," booklets such as *Between a Woman and Her God*, and educational series such as "The Really Good News: What the Bible Says About Sex."

Sex Information and Education Council of Canada (SIECCAN)
850 Coxwell Ave., Toronto, ON, M4C 5R1
(416) 466-5304
fax: (416) 778-0785
e-mail: sieccan@web.net
Web site: www.sieccan.org

SIECCAN is a national nonprofit organization established in 1964 to foster public and professional education about human sexuality. SIECCAN is dedicated to informing and educating the public and professionals about all aspects of human sexuality in order to support the positive integration of sexuality into people's lives. Its publications include the *Canadian Journal of Human Sexuality*, a quarterly, peer-reviewed journal; *Common Questions About Sexual Health Education*, a resource document published online; *Being Sexual: An Illustrated Series on Sexuality and Relationships*, a seventeen-booklet series to meet the educational needs of people with developmental disabilities or problems with language, learning, and communication.

BIBLIOGRAPHY

Books

Bill Albert, *With One Voice: America's Adults and Teens Sound Off About Teen Pregnancy*. Washington, DC: National Campaign to Prevent Teen and Unplanned Pregnancy, 2007.

Heather Corinna, *S.E.X: The All-You-Need-to-Know Progressive Sexuality Guide to Get You Through High School and College*. New York: Marlowe, 2007.

Heather Docalavich and Phyllis Livingston, *Youth Coping with Teen Pregnancy: Growing Up Fast*. Philadelphia: Mason Crest, 2008.

Ruth Graham and Sara R. Dormon, *I'm Pregnant—Now What?* Ventura, CA: Regal, 2004.

Saul D. Hoffman and Rebecca A. Maynard, *Kids Having Kids: Economic Costs & Social Consequences of Teen Pregnancy*. 2nd ed. Washington, DC: Urban Institute, 2008.

Institute for Youth Development, *Benefits of Delaying Sexual Debut*. Washington, DC: Institute for Youth Development, 2008.

Marty Klein, *America's War on Sexuality*. Westport, CT: Praeger, 2006.

Frederick S. Lane, *The Decency Wars: The Campaign to Cleanse American Culture*. Amherst, NY: Prometheus, 2006.

Sandra Augustyn Lawton, *Pregnancy Information for Teens: Health Tips About Teen Pregnancy and Teen Parenting*. Detroit: Omnigraphics, 2008.

June L. Leishman and James Moir, *Pre-teen and Teenage Pregnancy: A Twenty-first Century Reality*. Keswick, UK: M & K, 2007.

Kathy McCoy, *The Teenage Body Book*. New York: Hatherleigh, 2008.

Mark D. Regnerus, *Forbidden Fruit: Sex & Religion in the Lives of American Teenagers*. New York: Oxford University Press, 2007.

Youth Communication, *Teens Write About Preventing Pregnancy*. New York: Youth Communication, 2007.

Periodicals

Aisha Ali, "Teen Pregnancy: Not Just for the Lower Class and Underprivileged," *Los Angeles Examiner*, October 23, 2008. www .examiner.com.

Julie Baumgardner, "Don't Stop Giving Teens Good Advice," *Washington Times*, September 21, 2008.

Linnea Brown, "Hernando Teens Told Abstinence Is Only Way," *Hernando Today*, September 14, 2008. www.hernandotoday .com.

Charles E. Buban, "Tackling Teen Pregnancy with Anime-Inspired Comics," *Philadelphia Daily Inquirer*, August 8, 2008. www .inquirer.net.

David Crary, "Teen Motherhood: Celebrity Buzz Belies Its Cost," Associated Press, October 23, 2008.

Theodore Dalrymple, "A Nation of Paedophiles: If Sex with Children Is So Wicked, Why Are We Relaxed About Under-Age Pregnancy?" *New Statesman*, August 9, 2004.

Alexandra Rockey Fleming, "Mama Drama: Nancy Santiago Was a Fun-Loving Teenager. Then She Had a Baby. Suddenly, Life Changed—and Got Much Harder—in a Hurry," *Scholastic Choices*, January 2005.

Loretta Fulton, "No Easy Answers in Abilene's Teen Pregnancy Debate," *Abiline (TX) Reporter-News*, September 13, 2008. www .reporternews.com.

Miriam Gerace and Kate Short, "Looking at States with Parental Notification Laws," *Los Angeles Times*, October 23, 2008. www.latimes.com.

———, "Should Doctors Have to Notify Parents Before a Minor Receives an Abortion?" *Los Angeles Times*, October 22, 2008. www.latimes.com.

Jennifer Goodwin, "Teen Maternity: Birth Rate for Adolescents Is on the Rise Again After 15 Years of Decline," *San Diego Union-Tribune*, September 13, 2008. www.signonsandiego.com.

Cathy Gulli, Kate Lunau, Ken MacQueen, and Julia McKinnell, "Suddenly Teen Pregnancy Is Cool?" *Maclean's*, January 28, 2008.

Amanda Jenkins, "The Baby I'll Never Forget: Would I Ever Be Able to Forgive Myself for Having an Abortion?" *Christianity Today*, January 2006.

Christine C. Kim and Robert Rector, "Abstinence Education: Assessing the Evidence," *Executive Summary Backgrounder*, April 22, 2008.

Michael K. Magill and Ryan Wilcox, "Adolescent Pregnancy and Associated Risks; Not Just a Result of Maternal Age," *American Family Physician*, May 1, 2007.

Meg Meeker, "Sex Education on the Path to Revision? Bad Boys, 'Baby Daddies' and Lonely Girls Aren't in the Equation," *Washington Times*, August 28, 2008.

Newsday, "Cultural Boundaries Can Frustrate Teen-Pregnancy Counseling," October 15, 2007.

PR Newswire, "New Research Shows That Teens with Religious Parents and Friends More Likely to Delay Sexual Activity," November 16, 2005. prnewswire.com/public interest.

INDEX

Ireland, Amanda, 78

J
Johnston, Levi, 29
Jolie, Angelina, 33
Jones, Kortesha, 58
Journal of Adolescent Health, 8
Juno (film), 32, 59

K
Kaye, Keleen, 20
Kefalas, Maria, 6, 23, 78–79
Kids Having Kids (Hoffman
  and Maynard), 8
Kirby, Douglas, 87
Kirk, Carolyn, 13
Kizner, Scott, 36
Kline, Phill, 64, 65

L
Landen, Randy, 67
Landry, David, 11, 13
Lo, Shari, 82, 88

M
Mathmatica Policy Research,
  11
McCain, John, 40
McGovern, Chanda, 34
Men, adult
  are responsible for teen
    pregnancies, 58–62, 63–69
Moloney, Daniel P., 76

N
National Campaign to
  Prevent Teen and

Unplanned Pregnancy, 5, 15,
  59
New York Times (newspaper),
  86
Nisbet, Robert, 51
No Easy Answers (Kirby), 87

O
Oberman, Michelle, 65
Oldham, Lisa, 34–35
Omar, Hatim, 35, 36
Orr, Becky, 102

P
Palin, Bristol, 27, 29, 40,
  58–59, 71, 74
Palin, Sarah, 27, 29, 40–41,
  70–71
Parental consent
  abortions by minors and,
    90–94, 95–101
  contraceptives are prescribed
    without, 79, 80
Parker, Kim, 64, 65, 66
Patrick, Pat, 60
Perry, Rick, 96
Planned Parenthood, 94
Poor women
  are more likely to have
    unwanted pregnancies, 19
  cutbacks in contraceptive
    services for, 23–24
  views on children among, 6,
    78–79
Popma, Marlys, 41
Potter, Tim, 63
Poverty

PICTURE CREDITS

December 2010